THE TEARS OF 700 SOULS

PALMETTO
PUBLISHING
Charleston, SC
www.PalmettoPublishing.com

Hardcover ISBN: 979-8-8229-4879-2
Paperback ISBN: 979-8-8229-4880-8

THE
TEARS *of*
700 SOULS

PISTOL PETE

My First Love

My first love will be my last
I will love you more than gold
It will not be this world that I grab
It will be you that I hold
I will love you more than the sea
I will love you more than the sky
There is so much good in me
Take my hand and I'll teach you to fly
No love soars as high
No mind thinks of a girl as much as I

Will You

Will you be my fruit loop, will you be my cheerio
Will you be my lucky charm, cause I really love you
Will you be my strawberry, well you be my tomato
Will you be my raspberry, cause I still love you
Will you be my onion dip, will you be my Fritos
Will you be my only chip, cause I will love you
You are my time; you are my place
You are my air; you are my space
I do not lust for love, but I must, for love
If it's just because, I really truly love you

Next to You

I love the fragrant smell on your soft skin
But most of all, I love the heart you have within
You are prettier than a morning in June
One day we will spend a night on the moon
Just you, me, and the roses around us my lady
Not one rose, not two of those, nor three, but eighty
I love your sparkling eyes and silky hair
I'm interested in you, who is as cool as air

Time and time again I think about you
As the day begin, I think about you
You're as light as a bird's feather
You're as hot as summers weather
You are an angel whose face shines like the sun
If names were numbers, you'd be my only one

Friends Til the End

From the depths of the ocean to the top of the surface
I'll be your friend like there's no other purpose
From the root of the trees to the shine on the leaves
I'll be your friend like the birds and the bees
From the center of my heart to the thought in my mind
I'll be your friend because you are mine

Whatever it takes

Whatever it takes sunsets or sunrises
for you I'll give the unthinkable surprises
Red roses, sex, rich chocolates, and Valentine
whatever it takes to make you become mine
the movies, long nights, and sexual tangles
whatever it takes for you to be my beautiful Angel

The Gladiator

Sitting in the cold with a sword and a shield
Sitting in the cold with brutal wounds to heal
We fought till the last man
We fought till the enemies ran
My sword is bleeding with anger
My sword is proceeding with danger
There is no turning back

I must stay and prepare for an attack
Without love or care for my opponent
I'll ask with my sword how do you want it

In my arms

In my arms is where you should be
In my arms you will feel free
In my arms it won't be cold
In my arms it's you I'll hold
In my arms you will feel heat
In my arms your heart will beat
In my arms you will feel
I love so true and very real
In my arms you won't miss
The passionate feeling of an eternal kiss
In my arms I hope you'll be
Always and forever and for eternity

Count On Me

Count on me when you are down
Count on me to lift your sound
Count on me to lift you up
Count on me to fill your cup
Count on me when it is raining
Count on me for the love you're gaining
Count on me for any reason
Count on me throughout the season
Count on me my beautiful flower
Count on me at any minute of the hour
Count on me to love you forever
Count on me to make it all better
When things are too far and too hard to see
Trust in your heart and Count on me

Too Dark, Too Cold

Down the hill, high and low
The wind hollers yells and blows
The night is old of aging season
My mind is kind of so many reasons
I tried to find one seed of sunlight
But darkness is too black to love the light
One day I will find my everlasting light
But not today nor tonight

You

It is you who is willing to give your life
A burden you take you must sacrifice
It is you who is willing to let it all go
Before you leave there's one thing you should know
It is you whom I love, the love of my life
The pattern to all things our beloved sacrifice

So Cold

As the bright night Thunder crosses the shore
I'll be cold-hearted like I was before
The air was cold on that winter day
I'll remain lonely, sad, and grey
But as the eagle soars across the shore
I try and try for you once more
So cold, so lost of an internal frost
We cherish this pain; we pay the cost
I fly to you, with wings I sore
The aim is your heart, to love you forevermore
No matter the cost, no matter how bold
I will soar through the frost, through a winter so cold

Beautiful Flower

You are my beautiful flower; you will never die
I will always take care of you, I will try
I will feed you; I will water you I will shine on your face
I will cherish you; I Will love you, with God's giving grace
For every second, for every minute, and every time of the hour
I will always be there for you, my beautiful undying flower

The Beach

What a beautiful beach, so sandy and sweet
With sands of gold beneath my feet
The waves are calm and very high
And blue like the sky
The palm trees provide precious pleasures
And relaxing views of sensational measures
The glorious sun is an everlasting light
I would love to keep it in my sight
You are very beautiful my amazing view
The one that I would seek if only it is you

As The World Turns

As the world turns, so does my heart
Now that she's gone, I must turn to God
He is the only true love I've got
I should not have fell in love from the start
As the world turns, I turn cold
Now that she's gone, I must turn to ice
It is the only comfort I have that is sweet and nice
It's the only hand I will ever hold

I Could Wait Forever

Knowing me I could wait forever.
For the two of us to be together
No matter how soon no matter how late
I could hold on, I could wait
If you find someone else and he's a good mate
I could hold on I could wait
If you have kids and get old of age
I will still hold on I will still wait
Whatever happens bad or great
I will hold on I will wait
I would wait to be with you
No matter how long no matter how soon
Whether in January or in June
For me to be with you and for us to be together
I will wait for you; I will wait forever

Meakale

In her shell I could tell that she was shy and also frail
And in that pale skin of yours I saw the eyes parallel
I saw your grin and little chin and deep within, you loved me
The sweet perfume played its tune into my nose to consume
And at that hour I'd devour something pale like the moon
I chose the wrong way to treat such a lady, with mud I drug you there
And looking back I wished it daily to replay the moments that we shared
If I could do it all again, I'd buy a bottle just to spin
To choose you, and you alone; I'd write to you with my pen
I'd look into your eyes and kiss your lips
I'd whisper deep into your ears
I'd hold your today and hope for tomorrow
To treat you so special, but instead there's sorrow
The connection was special, the blood rushed to my heart
When I was with you, our eyes were in space
And in that face were your beautiful eyes of mars

And in that color, I could not erase
To you, my dear sweet Meakale, I hope to see you one day soon
And hope for my nose to once again, taste the scent of you to consume

Will You(2)

Will you be my life will you be my dream
Will you be my wife and my everything
Will you be my all will you be my flower
Will you answer my call at any minute of the hour
Will you be there for me to love
For me to care, will you be there

An Unknown Love

For every stair that we share will be a kiss to compare
When I look into your eyes, I see the truth and no lies
They sparkle so bright like the moon in the night
Your hair I'll compare to a bird's feather in the air
Your voice is like a bird I love to hear every word
For every kiss that I wish to give to you, but I miss
Your lips I dream are strawberries placed in cream
But your eyes are an adventurous disguise
When they rise there's a surprise about your dark sullen eyes
Your hugs we have not shared
But in the future, they will be compared
The sound of your voice is like the sound of the wind
I cannot see it, but I would love to hear it over and over again
Your beautiful eyes are the reason why
The reason that stars appear in the night sky
Your skin is like milk and as soft as silk
Your hands are warm things I want to hold
I'd rather have them than all the world's gold
With a rose I will enclose at the end of this note
But for a kiss I will compare to every stare that we share

Her Strength

You are the light of the ocean
You are the light in my hand
You are the light within my day
You are the light upon the sand
Like a green apple I was sour
I felt this way until that hour
I saw a lovely and beautiful flower
Which turned me sweet with all of her power

Split Personality

When he is with me there is no void
But over the telephone he is paranoid
When he is touching me I feel electric
But over the telephone he is more domestic
His kisses are everlasting and warm to my soul
But when we're not face to face and my heart bears a hole
I am but a flower a beautiful flower
Sweet and right and not sour
He calls me these things but dares not prove
He is quick to stand still but not to move
Why so much pain and so much pride
You never show your face, You just hide
Show me what I've missed when we first met
The moment in heaven that I'll never forget

A Long Time is Gone

A long time ago when there was a tree, is now a house as you can see
A long time ago when there was a stream, is now a man's dwelling and
newfound dream
A long time ago when there were two, Is now billions and billions of all of you
A long time ago when there was slavery, is now freedom courage and
bravery

A long time ago when there was respect, is now heartbreak and the feeling of regret
A long time ago when there was discipline, is now a generation who is not listening
A long time ago when there was a book, is now television and movies life took
A long time ago when there was love, is replaced with something that we call a hug
But there is something we will never change, life and death will always remain

My Love

I do not love you for your smile
nor by your hair compares the Nile
I do not love you for your hand
nor by your feet are grains of sand
I do not love you for your eyes
nor by your face compares the skies
I do not love you for your breast
know about your heart which is the fairest
I do not love you for your Pearl
nor by your jewel compares the world
but I do love you for who you are
the love of my life my shooting star

My Haunted Past

From what happened in my past is happening again
not to me but by my beautiful, sweet friend
my friend is a girl who has a lover
and to me he is like my blood brother
but what long ago has happened to me
is happening now in a nightmare's dream
she wants to stay but he pushes away
she wants to love but instead he shoves
so I am here so the fear in her won't last
as it did long ago in my haunted past

The Divided Paper

God has given us a heart to feel of love and pain that is very real
three years ago, I met a girl, she meant more to me than anything in the
world
the first time seeing her was August 16th, 2004
I'd never seen a glass as fragile as her before
she was shy but pretty as the new day
and her beauty was like the month of may
on the 15th of December she gave me something
I wanted her love if only that one thing
as shy as I was, I didn't say
I love you dear girl every single day
why didn't I? I'll never know
I'll never forget how her eyes did glow
so, as God said love your neighbor
I will love my neighbor, and this divided paper.

My Dream

As unexpected as this may seem
I write to you of what I dreamed
as soon as I woke up, I started to write
about what I dreamed of you last night
there was a dream in my head
you were lying in my bed
I saw a tear come from your eye
and at that moment I started to cry
because God has given me the reality of you
of all my dreams you came true
you were so cold I held you tight
to keep you warm all through the night
so, with you beside me and I beside you
I thank the Lord that my dream came true.

About a girl that I knew

I hope you find this rhyme amusing; I hope it won't be too confusing
this story is about a girl I saw, she's pretty and white but that's not all
I met her on the night of New Year's Eve, she likes Katt Williams and
Keanu Reeves
she said they are hot like the other guys she mentioned
but to me it sounds like a teen crush convention
she loves to eat shredded cheese and also carrots
and if I wanted some, she would probably share it
her three future kids are G L and R
and when summer comes, she will get a car
her girlfriend's names are Lindsey Brittany and others
her boyfriend's names are Mario and Luigi the Mario brothers
she loves to dance she loves to party, she loves to drink orange juice with
Bacardi
her hair is brown and her eyes are too, well I didn't see her eyes did you
she's going to be a nurse and I can't wait, because whenever I'm hurt she
will operate
she loves to go shopping for shoes and clothes
she is the only flower that they call a rose
Billie Jean is really not my girl she is just a girl who wishes I was the one,
but her kid is not my son
but enough of the talk and enough of the dilly dally
her name is not Billy her name is really Calli
I hope you found this rhyme amusing and I hope it wasn't too confusing

The Pitcher's Mound

I have no friends I am all alone, with dirt around me I call it my home
they step on me when I am clean, sometimes it makes me cry and also
scream
I cannot move or go where I please, I am the pitcher's mound, please have
mercy on me

Shackles

you broke my heart you broke my dreams no break these shackles and set me free
all I ever wanted was my dream to come true
that's all I ever wanted I wanted you
I can hear you from the past, when you looked at me and laughed
I'm writing this to let you know, I found my love so let me go
you broke my heart you broke my dream
and I'll break these shackles and let me be

Life has no limits

I can't live without you it would be death
if life were ever so true then I would have no breath
so we must remain together you hear and I near forever
the breeze will not blow this love away
nor the fear that I had of yesterday
I will not hide my love as I did before
I will close fears gates and open Love's door
it would be death to live without you
if so, life would be untrue
so, we must remain together
with you here and I near, forever

The Artist

Brown, red, yellow or white, which of these colors will he use tonight
with a stroke of his brush, it appears
as beautiful as ever, like music to my ears
her beautiful name is the reason I exist
and God is her creator and an illustrative artist

Times Like This

It's times like this I need you here
I'd hold you tight all through the night

I'll never let go, you're my only hope
my love I'll prove your heart will move
and I will move more closer to you
it's times like this I have to write
my love is pure it must endure
I feel so alive when I look into your eyes
My uncontrollable flame is the fire to my desire
and it is only you whom I'll always admire

The Thought of You

As the wind blows on the trees
my lonely words will blow on thee
As the leaves fall from the trees
I fall for you on bended knee
there was a message sent to me
a message that made me feel so free
you are the sun which sets by the sea
and also, the stars that revolves around me
the moment that I saw you walk past me
I had to make this come to be
and with my words expressing truth
all right tonight with the thought of you

What Must I Do

What must I do to be with you
I know you are a peach, and I am blue
but I love you so and this is true
please hear my call among all the others
I will be your night and one true lover
they may say that all of us are the same
but I am the true pitcher for your frame
if I can't have you then tell me why
I will give you the world I will try
what must I do to be with you

must I call upon you when feeling low
to lift your eyes for they glow
Must I hold you tight and take you there
to a high place, a place in the air
I know you are a peach, and I am blue
but I'd do anything to be with you

If You Do Want To Know

The place wherein falls the snow
Or where a rose bud will grow
Or of the waterfalls below
If you do want to see
A red, rosy cheek
A strawberry placed in cream
Or the truth of my everlasting dreams
If you wish to see the sky
And do not know the reason why
Or how a beauty soars so high
Then look in the mirror with both eyes

If They Only Knew

If they only knew what my heart knew
If they only knew what my pencil drew
If they only knew why the sky is blue
If they only knew how flowers bloom
If they only knew why the morning is new
If they only knew that one made two
If they only knew why the dove flew
If they only knew how the love grew
If they only knew of this beautiful view
If they only knew that these words give a clue
If they only knew that these days are few
If they only knew how my dreams came true

If they only knew what my heart will do
If they only knew that I truly love you

Every Season with You

In the summer if you sleep
I'll slumber by your feet
In the winter by the fire
I will center my desire
In the spring you will walk
Through my dreams my love will talk
In the fall we will stand
With you as my girl and I as your man
Spending every season with you and only you
Is something I will always love to do

The Digger

I dug a hole that is very deep
for my love I vow to keep
with my pen I dig this hole
for her heart and for her soul
I've dug other holes but none so low
this particular one continues to grow
I'm stuck in a hole and will never leave
but there is a treasure I must receive
I'm so close; I must remain
a digger of love for life is her name

Friends for Eternity

In love and trust I have found a friend, and that is why this letter I send
she is so demanding but yet so sweet, thank you God for two hearts to meet
it is good to have a friend who really cares, to always know that she will be there
we must not judge but if it be me, an Angel from heaven is what I see

if you but think that this poem is dumb, cut my fingers for they are numb
but if you like what you see, then plant a seed to possess a tree
a tree of love and trust we'll be, friends forever and for eternity

The Growth of my Dreams

My heart is growing every day, of knowledge and love in every way
Two hearts belong together, two hearts are better than never
I believe in you; do you believe in me
This road that I take is too hard to see
I dreamed about you again last night
Your beautiful eyes were in my sight
With soft dark hair your stare was dared, but I had to look because I cared
Without words but only glances, the more I stare my love enhances
With this dream that I see, I wish for it to be reality

When I cry, I die

When I cry, I die, my life of love is a lie
When I try I am denied, Of this truth I should not have lied
when I fly the dream of dream is denied
when I cry my tears drown me and I die

How

How does the wind move a fallen leaf
sometimes so sudden and also brief
how does the clouds appear as they are
or the undying brightness of a single star
how does the sunshine with desire
Does it too possess an uncontrollable fire
how does a bird fly with its wings
or a flower that blooms when it is spring
how does the moon transform so
to fill the night with the heavenly glow
how does a raindrop fall from the sky

as though a tear would fall from an eye
how is such a heart so fragile and so sweet
a girl who is beauty compares to each heartbeat

Never stop believing

Believe in yourself to do anything
is in you to do many things
your dreams will come true
believe it and it will happen to you
you may fall in the process
but stand tall for there is progress
don't stop, God is here
don't stop, he is near
you can do anything if you believe
Never give up on your destiny.
your dreams will come true
if you believe in you
don't fall down don't fail to see
you have to see yourself as you wish to be
your voice makes a beautiful song
hearing you speak makes me strong
with all that you wish to come true or exist
maybe this and never lasting kiss
a kiss of faith, love, and trust
it is we who must believe in us

Lean on Me

When you are in need of a friend, call on me for I am him
When you are reaching out for a hand, sail your tears to my land
When you are lonely and no one cares, come to my arms for they are there
You are a miracle from the month of May, and I will be there to love you
everyday
Your storm will be my light and sunshine
Your troubles will be no more yours, but they will be mine

You will fill pain no more, like you used to feel before
I will show you, I will be, your everlasting shoulder so lean on me

A Prayer

With this prayer I pray tonight, I pray to say whatever is right
As you're sleeping in your bed, I send my words for your soul to be fed
You are the patient, and he is the med, I pray this message will heal your head
Sleeping may do it as well as prayer. A prayer for one to whom I care
So, with this message of prayer I write I'll pray, I'll dream, I'll say goodnight

My Beautiful Butterfly

I love the stars and the moon, as red as mars, my love came soon
I love the ocean and the sea, a love explosion for you and me
I love your cheeks and your eyes, and when you speak my anger dies
As a mystery or a lover, I will whisper, "there is no other"
I love your glimmer and your color; my love will enter for yours to uncover
With your wings you fly so high, from the trees to the sky
How did your beauty transform so
From a caterpillar to a colorful glow
Every time it snows your beauty gradually grows
What I compare is more than a rose
Even though you have this mutual other guy
You will always be my beautiful butterfly

My Gift

My gift, I have to use it
A golden gift, I won't refuse it
If I stop then I will lose it
But I won't, I will pursue it
I will never abuse it
I did not choose it
But with God's sweet music
I will use it

Never Quit Dreaming

If you want to keep her forever, create a small but deep love letter
If you want her eyes in yours, a word in rhyme will do it of course
If you fear of a disappointing denial, look into her eyes and give her a smile
You have her attention, now gain her trust, with a smile, or with true love
If her parents deny your dream, let them know that your love is a stream
If she feels lost or stuck in a maze, write a poem for her eyes to gaze
A denial may feel like she never cared, but love was there when she stared
And now you feel hate for the world, because of one beautiful girl
It is not her decision, but it is her folks
"I am a human being, not a hoax"
She says that she likes me because I am sweet
But you sent me a message and she does not speak
Is she scared, does she even care
I thought she would care and always be there
Some days I feel like giving up the fight, but I can't relive that heart-breaking night
Some days I sit and think of her, with a glimpse so quick it feels like a blur
Why avoid me like this, why not see my heart
I don't think I can dream again, so with this nightmare, I pretend
I'll pretend that we are together, two lovers, in love forever

The Colors of a Friend

The red sun, the green sea, the purple sky is in thee
A silver star, a blue day, a white flower appeared in May
Your red cheeks, your green stems, your Purple Heart create your lens
A silver star, a blue goodbye, a bright white smile to fill the sky

I Tried So Hard

I tried so hard to gain her trust, I succeeded well and swept the dust
I tried so hard to show her love, I succeeded well with an unforgettable hug
I tried so hard to share my heart, I succeeded well, we will never part
I tried so hard to be with her, I failed completely of what we were

I tried so hard to live my life, but love stabbed me with a knife
I tried so hard to prove to her better, more than she'll know, with a love letter
I tried so hard to heal my pain. And I did but it came back again
Should I live or should I die, why should I even try?
I can't give up on my life, so with prayer I'll pray tonight
Please dear Lord, touch my soul, so that love and peace will make me whole.

My Long-Ago Love

It's more than her eyes and more than her voice
The smell of her hair, my love has no choice
Her heart is in mine, she is my dream
The sweetness of her lips, a cherry placed in cream
Her eyes struck me first, then her dark brown hair
As hot as the sun, as cool as the air
Her complexion is compared to every beat
The beat of my heart, the love above my feet
Her hands are warm and soft to the touch
But if she only knew that I loved her so much
Why should I remove such a star from my sky
When she is the brightest with beauty so high
She has a kiss which compares to the sea
But this heavenly experience occurred in a dream
She is my dream, she is my shore
I'll love her for eternity, and forever more

When I First Saw Her

Once upon a time, when it was dark and cold
My eyes were young, but my legs were old
So, with my eyes I saw a light
Once upon a time, on a cold summer night
It appeared from the darkness of my burning eyes
And into my heart so it may rise

With the doors slowly closing
A light appeared and continued glowing
Then suddenly, my legs were full of life
Because of this miraculously beautiful light
She spoke to my heart with a voice so new
I've never heard such a voice nor seen such a view
When she smiled, I felt her joy
A gift from a lovely girl to a sweet boy
When her eyes met mine, my heart had stuttered
I wanted to speak but I just muttered
She took my breath but gave me light
Once upon a dark and cold summer night

Call Me

When you are feeling so alone
When someone evil has done you wrong
When life is too hard to carry on
When you are feeling weak and not strong
When it seems, all hope is gone
When there's no music left to this song
When you're feeling sick in your home
When a short story is never too long
Grab your mobile and call my phone
I will tell you, "You're not alone"

Hold on to love

Tomorrow never comes for dreamers today
It comes in your thoughts and also your stay
Fear in some is fear in all
Fear for one will cause the fall
It hurts deep inside when you're left alone
To live, to cry, to die at home
A rose I loved, a rose I drew
Where is that rose, if only I knew

Never give up on your one true wish
Find your true lover and gain a kiss
Life is love, pain, and more
Open your heart, close hate's door
Desire and passion will venture furthermore
I'll close hate's gate and open love's door

Wishing

Please let me see her again
I miss the hug of a dear friend
I wish that I could turn back time
Please dear Lord, ease my mind
I wish upon a fallen star
I wish, I hope, I dream afar
I'm wishing to one day see her again
Dear Heavenly Father, please tell me when

Her Heart

How fast, how warm, how soft, how calm
How loved, ho dear, it is sweet music to my ear
So fragile, so bright, with feelings of delight
With a beat so right, I'm blessed on this night
To be next to you, is all that I want to do
And where I want to be, with you for eternity

I Do Not Know Anymore

I'm crying with every word that I write
I miss you dearly, especially tonight
Your feelings are my advantage towards survival
Call upon me and I will come to you
I can't wait another day for your arrival
Thinking of you day and night is what I do
Sometimes It's hard to breathe knowing you're gone

But I have to face the fact and do what was said
You told me that I deserve more and to move on
For every word on his page, I've cried, so you've read

Writing in my Bed
Where I dream, where I sleep
I write tonight, tonight I dream
Where I think, where I cry
I write tonight, tonight I think
Where I love, where I hate
I write tonight, tonight I love
Where I live, where I die
I write tonight, tonight I live
Where I write, where I might
Receive a message, while I write

Something or Nothing
Snow is white, night is black
But up and away there lives a glow
Kisses are wet, yet hugs are warm
But dreams so blessed bears our wishes
Desire in my heart, part of my love
But she can never die from it, like fire
She is my dear, near my future
But this is a dream that I see
I have a wish, it is my dream
Will it live or will it die

Walk Away
Do not stay in a place that would cause death
Walk away and keep your breath
Walk away from the darkness of pain
Do not stay in a place where there is rain

Time is meant to feel emotions
Love is meant to be for lovers
Walk away from hatred my sisters and brothers.

If I Ever Hate Again

If I ever hate again, I will feel alone
Nobody to comfort me, nobody, no home
Not a bed, nor a chair, not a look, nor a stare
Not a friend, nor a lover, not a sister, nor a brother
If I ever hate again, I will feel every cloudy day
Nobody to shine on me, nobody, on a day so grey
Not a cat, nor a dog, not a princess, nor a frog
Not a boy, nor a girl, no one in this lonely world
If I ever hate again, it would be the end

I Am Here

In the cold without a coat
Or love to warm your solid iced soul
You lifted your legs to gain more faith
On a night so grey and dark to lay
You start to walk, then run cross country
To search, to seek, it's me you're hunting
One stumble to fall you fell on the floor
I am here for you; you'll fall no more

What Am I

I am nothing, I do not exist in this world
This life is real but not to me
I am nothing but a nightmare
I tried to love, I tried to hate, I tried
I'm tired of trying, I feel nothing
I am nothing, I care about nothing
I am alone and on my own

I have no friends, nor do I have enemies
I have nothing; I have nobody; I am on my own
I'm alone. I do not exist in this world
I am me; I am dead, I am a nightmare
I am nothing

A Letter of Love

You appeared to me from the sky
An angel sent by the one who sits on high
It was at that moment I started to imagine
If life, love, and dreams could happen
I looked into your eyes to see the springs grass
Thank you, dear love; I've found you at last
I was all alone I was down and out
You saved my soul, with faith I am bold
You came into my life like the speed of light
with love so fast, with love so right
I cried so hard; I was stuck in my mind
But deep down inside there was you; your mine
You're my day. My beautiful wife
Without you I can't be me
To have found you at last, my destiny
Thank you, God, for this cup I hold
For an angel so sweet, she's filled my soul
To have found you at last, to love you forever
To know more about a girl, read this love letter

My Wife

As I sit on the weight of the world
I wait patiently on a call from a girl
Her name is unknown, but she'll be my wife
And while I wait, I'll write on this night
She's somewhere out there; the love of my life
My darling angel, my beautiful wife

Imagination of Life

Paradise is in my sight
A view of a beach with pebbles and trees
The moon is grey in the night
The air blows a cool breaths breeze
Freshwater honeycombs and friendly weather
Sunshine raindrops and love forever
Dark days, lonely nights, and also pain
But when light appears faith is gained
Bright nights, sunny lights, and bright days
Right left time itself would remain always

My Only Hope

You are my only hope that I have in life
My words you create are built on ice
I'm as cold as the ocean which my tears have made
I'm as dead as the words written on my grave
You are the shelter of my fears I had of being me
You've given my hands an art which no one can see
Your tongue speaks my words as the grey day
I was born to hold you since the 5th of may
I will let you go for now and silently fade away
And hope to one day see you again my dear sweet Alize

As Sweet As Sweet

Chocolate covered coated candy
Swallows the sweet taste of marshmallow clouds
Tears, raindrops, smiles, sunshine
Fine wine at 9:00 behind the diner's line
This sweet taste of life
Freedom, we have a life to live
Love it well as sweet as sweet
As sweet as sweet my life I love

Valentine's Day

On a day with time to spare
On a day with love to share
A heart for you a heart for me
A heart for everyone to see
To dream of her to dream of life
To dream of you as my wife
A gift that was given a gift from the heart
I'm glad you're here leaving I'm glad our love cannot part
To part my Valentine
To part my heart
To love forever to love what's mine
My beautiful and beloved Valentine

Abstract

I am the world you wish to see
A dream with shackles to set you free
I am the tree you grow up on
A fruit field to weigh a ton
I am the page you wish to read
A word written for you to see
A view seen on paper to learn
I feel your thoughts to twist so turn
A world of life to give to others
I am a writer your heart's true lover
The heart so sweet to taste my tongue
A bite the fruit which made me young

Silver Spoon

I'm rich in faith but poor in doubt
I'm rich in love but poor in hate
I'm poor in present but rich in memory
And poor being dead and rich being alive

Where is my place in this world
Rich or poor I'm alone but loved

A cold sweater

I put it on to show you I am alive
I wear it proudly its Celsius disguise
As cold a cloth my heart is melting
It tears away my dark sides sheltering
I stand by the fire to warm my face
This sweater is ice in a winter-filled place
Would I even care if my sweater was old
I'm alone in linen and frozen so cold

Forever in love

The girl of my dreams my beautiful light
The shine on my face my star at night
The beat to my heart fast or slow
The rise of the sun a beautiful glow
To find you at last is like the start of something new
With me as your son and you as my dew
I'll give you the stars if you give me the moon
This love came quick but not too soon
You're the voice in my mind which causes me to speak
The pieces to the puzzle which made me complete
I hope you're the one the love of my life
The girl I call upon the one who will be my wife
I'll treat you with respect and give you my all
I am your summers spring and your winter fall
You say that I am different from the rest
I want to give you more for you and nothing less
The reason that I have you is the same that I care
Call me when you need me, and I will be there
Now that I have you, I am never letting go
Remain my winter and my breeze and I'll stay your winter snow

To Sit and Not Walk

This day is windy and cold, with Winter fresh gum freezing my soul
The mind I have is foolish but sharp, so is my pencil the tune of a Harp
Men are walking and carrying tables, open the legs of the dearly disabled

A Love Letter 2

If I had one wish, I would wish to have wings
To fly to you every season summer fall winter and spring
You are so beautiful to me inside and out
I want you forever I want you right now
To have you in my arms I'd hold you tight
Feeling your heartbeat every day and every night
You are the one the girl of my dreams
With the sign in my sky the ice in my cream
The cream in my crop the apple of my eye
With you in my life I can only feel but high
No need for wings you are here with me
The center of my heart which made me complete
I may not have much but what I have to give to you
My words my all and something new
You've been hurt before and so have I
But I will not break your heart nor tell a lie
But what I will do is make you smile
I'll be in your thoughts for more than a while
You are sweet and amazing you are beautiful and kind
Thank you sweet for being only mine
I want to feel your heart I want to feel your skin
I want to feel your body and everything within
I want you in my future and forever in my life
Possibly as my queen and hopefully my wife
Dear sweet love: you're the reason I write
You are the sun in my day you are the moon in my night
Thank you for existing and thank you for being mine
This love is a given that was not hard to find

Torture in Heaven

Caught in a light with a beautiful angel
A glimpse of love but coiled in tangles
I held her there, in a place new to me
But sinned my salvage unspiritual to thee
She took my love and became my God
I worshiped her, I had no pride
I speak of a girl who was in my past
I loved her more than I did myself
I wanted this love to forever last
But love has sin to poison my health
Today I see hate and darkness
And tomorrow maybe light will part us

Alone

I remember when we were all small, when the grass was green but that's not all
I remember her well I remember it all, I'm just waiting on a call but that's not all
I remember the days playing tag, the fun that we had without a dad
I remember the tears and I remember the fights, All through the night I remember it alright
I remember her name they're saying but different too
If I remember correctly, she said I love you
I wish I could remember you ghosts are unseen
I wish that you would only appear to me more than a nightmares dream
A dream of someone who will always be there
But I wake to discover another nightmare

Farewell

I know you will not care about this letter
But I want to say sorry to make things better
I know that we are no longer friends
But I don't want to call it an end
There's so much more I wanted to know

Before the day I let you go
I wrote this farewell for you to keep
To store in your heart very deep
I'll never forget the conversations we had
Even if they were sometimes bad
If there's a memory, I'll never lose
It would be the night I sat beside you
I know on that night I didn't talk
It wasn't because of you; it was my fault
I will miss the sound of your beautiful voice
It always made a lovely noise
I will miss the glow of your pretty brown eyes
They shine so bright like stars in the sky
There's something else that I will miss
The dream of me giving you a kiss
Your lips were soft, calm and still
But the kiss was aggressive and ready to feel
I will miss the hugs we shared
Two hearts together, we both cared
I will remember the night we first me
It was New Year's Eve and I'll never forget
Dear sweet love of this sad depart
You will always be a part of my heart
You say that we are no longer friends
But to gain your love, this letter I send

My World

Roses are blue, violets are red
This is a world stuck in my head
The moon is gold, the sun is grey
It will be cold in the month of May
Winter is hot, summer is cold
The rich lives in half
The poor lived in whole
A dog meows, a cat barks

The night is bright, the day is dark
The sand is blue, the ocean is white
A cowboy is black, a rapper is white
The women are the king, the man is the queen
Men put on lipstick and women shaving cream
The good are criminals, the cops are too
The bad are good and so are you
Preps are ghetto, black people are proper
Medicine kills just like doctors
The children are sweet, Kool-Aid is sour
Gas prices go down at every minute of the hour
Girls are treated with all deserved respects
At every zoo there's a Jurassic Park T-Rex
Oprah's poor, but I am rich
PB&J is not a sandwich
This is my world, the opposite of yours
And do we have gentleman, well yes, of course
Every flower is named after a girl
But I am the one who controls this world

Beauty

There is a field in your face
Where white lilies and red roses grow
A heavenly paradise is that place
Wherein, pure and faithful falls the snow
You are like a summer's day
You're prettier than a morning June
You are the reason flowers bloom in May
You are the glow that appears on the moon
Your voice is like a bird
A song recorded in my mind
I memorize every word
I remember every line
I'm glad that he made you

As my friend and more
I never saw a sweeter face
Then that I stood before

The Cream in my Coffee
You are my sugar; you are my lover
You are my day with the lightest color
You are the light in my darkness
You are sweet, you are bright
You are what guides me through the night
You are my mixture, a perfect picture
It is easy and not hard to see
You are the cream in my coffee

Writing About Us
My paper is white, my ink is black
Segregation is over, debating the fact
To write my thoughts, why think these things
I only write what my mind may bring

Tonight's Dream
Tonight, let's lie under the stars
So, I can look into your eyes as mars
Your heart beats fast of the sound of a drum
Let's hold hands until the moist rises upon
Let's talk of love, our love fore each other
Caught in the moment until the rain becomes our weather
I will remember this moment with you forever
If it were only true; to leave you never
What you read may but seem
As a thought but only a dream

So Hard To Love

When you think of a girl, and you wish upon a star
How far do we go to show who we are
How much to impress, how long does it take
Do you look in her heart or stare at her face
She escapes the love, which was once broken
It kills to be hurt by the one who's been chosen

Thinking of You

I loved them all
Every girl that looked my way
I loved them all
She was beautiful that day
I miss you
I'm sorry for not treating you like a queen
I miss her
I see her always when I dream
I must not let her go, for I only have one life
So, with a fist full of ink, I write to you tonight
Why couldn't you see how much I cared
My love for you will last, even in heaven
Why do you not understand the tears that we've shared
I cried with raindrops which were given
I will never forget what you've placed in my heart
I will never forget he first time
The first time seeing the eyes of stars
I will always remember you when you were mine

Deep Down Below, Dirty Demons Blow

Faithful thoughts gazed upon me
With nothing frozen but I me and space
There have been many things talked about

But nothing as delicate as her face
A dove flew and angels sing with heaven sight starting to face
The joker, prince, king, nor queen could not breath to lay the spade
I sit and wonder if love grows close or faraway, I dare not look
My heart is cold and full of love, of pain and ice, the road I took
I'm in a web of hell and tangles
To find my way in a coil
This harvest of peace within my drams
It grows to cause my eyes to boil
It's Wednesday morning, the birds are dead
And the trees are gone with he wind
If life exists, I'd kiss her lips
But love has damaged my heart instead
In class I write, despite the day
My soul is cold, I cannot breath
With seconds to live, I think of her name
Before I shatter with broken wings
I wake to find darkness gone; it light exits in my pen
Faith has given me love to find
My dearest and beloved beautiful friend

Whatever May Come
I wake up to see your beautiful face
A message of such to gaze a view
A drawing sketched to never erase
The spark of light that is in you
Voices traded and heart well
My heart leaped to hear her speak
A night of joy which caused a spell
To make my heart forget to beat
My eyes searched to find that light
But darkness grew day by day
No more sun, my heart to fight
To carry on and continue to breathe
I give my heart shattered in two

I give my story, my words replay
I only wish to dream of you
An angel I heard that night in May

Love

In a life full of desire, there is so much more
We dare not search to find the reason what we need it for
The weight of the world is held in the start
But paradise is what means a lot to my heart
Why build treasures and riches upon this ground
When there is life to be found, do not fall down
Stand with both feet and lift a lost child
What's so hard about the task when the question is how
Faith is the key and hope is unseen
But if you know it is there, love will proceed
We dare not search to find what we need if for
But with life full of love, there will always be more

Everything

All that I remember about her is everything
This feeling inside of me will never change
We fell from the moon that night
How could darkness overtake the light
How could a seed turn into a tree
It fades away like a broken dream
She grew into my heart with something new
Without her love my day are few
The days go by, yet memories remain
All that I remember about her is everything

You

Without you I am lost
Without you I am incomplete

If I could take it all back, I'd pay the cost
If I could see you again, I'd say "sorry"
Without you my heart was whole
If I could see you, I'd cry
If I could see you again my love would show
If there is anything I could do
I'd do it all just for "you"

Tearing Me Apart

Why should I call you baby
Why so we act a fool
Why are we so crazy
I'm so crazy about you
I try to please you daily
But then you turn so cruel
Why do you remain my baby
It's because I'm lost without you

Love Struck

You are more than what they say
Words cannot compare to your beautiful face
You are a flower which blooms in May
To touch your heart would be a wonderful embrace
You are beautiful inside and out
An amazing angel only lights control
If anything, it'd be you I'd hold
I do not know you, yet I gain your heart
To take this journey is where we will start
You spoke our words; my breath was taken
With a voice so pure, my ears were shaken
I looked into your eyes and saw the sun
I held your hand, and we became one
With the sun now setting and with something missing
I turned to your face, and we started kissing

Haley

There was once a heart I could not take
A heart so cold it could not melt
So strong and stubborn it could not break
Because of something sad that I felt
I touched the torcher and the hurt
From a body so cruel and full of hate
I picked her up from the dirt
I cleansed her mind to take hate away
With love now showing, I abandoned it all
With tears of hurt her heart did fall
She bled by a lie, the stain of pain
Then I said "goodbye", I'll never see you again

That Place

Take me to a place where life exists
A paradise so pleasant that's better than this
A place of love I hope not to miss
Had to follow you there but not because of that place
But because of the life you share and your beautiful face
I go anywhere as long as it's with you
Take me to a place where dreams come true
Where paradise is pleasant, and love is new
I'd go to that place because it is you that I choose

You and Me

In a place of walls with no light to see
A world of halls for only you and me
A surrounded cell with crowded dreams
Trapped in a spell is what it seems
One night of light, I reached for more

And yet I found the love that I was searching for
So bright a star, so beautiful to see
I'll never forget the night when it was you and me

Once Upon a Night 2

Once Upon a night a night so sweet
A night so unexpected she made my world complete
my illusion of love with something unseen
a world so silent and to sleep so deep
Once Upon a night and native darkness
I thought she was the one, but she left me heartless
Once Upon a night a night of broken dreams
I guess being alone it's not as bad as it seems
without the sign my sight is gone
Once Upon a night all alone
a night of sad tears, a night of darkness
the night my love abandoned me and left me heartless

Thinking of You

I cannot sleep you are on my mind
I think of you a lot I think of you all the time
on nights like this I'm torn in two
On nights like this I want to be with you
all right tonight to put a smile on your face
a sight so sweet a sight I'll never erase
I'm not a writer but attempt this letter
the thought of you always makes me feel better
when I think of you, I think of a rose in a garden full of life
a beautiful sweet rose such a rose I call my wife
when I think of you my skin crawls to want you so bad
I can taste you and when I touch you the thought of you will be all that I
have

DR3A.M.

3 A.M. and I cannot sleep
I close my eyes, but I cannot dream
I toss and turn and think of you
I write tonight of something true
it is 3 A.M. and I am awake
I write to say my body aches
To think of you kills my pain
I write about a girl from long ago
An angel that I used to know
A dream I wish to dream tonight
If only I could close my eyes
It's 3 A.M. so I'll try to sleep
I'll close my eyes hoping to dream
To dream of the past to dream of you
hoping one day it would all come true

Summer Love

Under a tree in the summer, I would love to hold you as you sleep
I would hold you tight on that night, and whisper in your ear something sweet
You are beautiful and also true, you're precious to me you are something new
I hope that we will be together. a moment that we have under this tree
I hope will last always and for eternity

Me

Blue, black, purple and brown
I bare this skin so why do you frown
why cast me away from the color of white
call me darkness for I am the night
you look upon me with a face so cruel
but I am the path and the richness of all jewels
you stare and you curse me from the day of my birth
to look up on me to gaze into my eyes, do you know what I am worth

Love So Unexpected

Of all the strangers who stand by my feet
It is you my dear rose who is beautiful and sweet
You're precious it's stems that reach out to me
And peddles so pure, creatures let me be
With something so new you have filled my soul
Of all the beautiful strangers you have made me whole

Night Love

So beautiful, so sweet; you are more than what is written
So precious, so loved; it is my heart that I am giving
You are beautiful and also amazing; you are every word that I am saying
You are my love, my beautiful light; you are the reason I write tonight

All of Her

Make her feel special and lift her above your feet
Hold her tight like there's no tomorrow, and then you will be complete
Instead of feeling hurt or a winter's pain, there will be love to gain
instead of a push or a shove you will feel her tender love
Instead of the darkness or a nightmare
You will see that she truly cares
In all that is said, and some may believe it's true
Love is all that I have, Love is all that I will do

In this room

In this room are many things
To vision us all on a string
To place my head upon a stand
In this room bears my hand
In this room are my words
To listen well of what's been heard
To tear this page to build my strength

In this room I will repent
In this room there is age
To grasp this sheet with led of rage
To learn why hearts hurt today
In this room where I will stay
Away from hurt, harm, or pain
In this room I live again

Should I Write

Should I write about tomorrow when the day is new
Or should I write about tonight about me and you
Should I write with my pencil or with my pen
Or with your heart, your beautiful soul, to show my feelings within

Dear Donna

I know that you will care about this letter, I want to say sorry to make
things better
I know that we will always be friends, and that is why this letter I send
I wrote his letter for you to keep; to store in your heart very deep
I will never forget that day at the store. It was you whom I was looking for
When I saw your face, I saw your smile, a smile I'll miss for more than a while
We talked for a minute, and you started to laugh
"Can you clean my car and steal a hubcap?"
I cleaned her car and at Burger King we ate; It was cheap but a romantic date
If there's a memory I will never lose, it would be the night at the animal
zoo
You saw the elephants and I saw your smile, and that is something I'll miss
for a while
I will always remember the times we've shared; good or bad, we both cared
I will remember the day when two became one, it was the 10th of
September when we begun
This story is the beginning and not a depart, for you will always be my
Minnie, a part of my heart

My Dear Friend

The love that we share will never tear
and that is why I prepare this note for you
awake every morning to see you there
apart from your heart I'll never do
with laughter and joy, we share this cloud
the place in the sky I've never been
if you were gone, I would cry so loud
remain here with me my darling friend.

Lady In My Life

You may not care about this letter, but I wrote it for you to make things better
there were more things I wanted to know, before the day I let you go
I miss your kiss and I miss your touch, to think of your name is the reason I blush
locked in a cell to keep us apart, but you always have the key to my heart
no matter where you are and no matter where you go
you'll always be the one who gave my heart a glow
the rainbow in my eyes wear waterfalls flow
you always be the Angel who laid in my snow
the sound of your voice was like the sound of a bird
I remember every line and also every word
I remember your love I remembered your smile
I think of you constantly, but it has been a while
what we had was something very real
I love only you and I could ever feel
you were everything good in me, my heart and soul
the missing piece to my puzzle which made me whole
dear sweet beauty before you disappear
there is something that I would love for you to hear
this letter I give like tears from my eyes
I'll give you my love this one last time
I close my eyes to see your face, a sight so sweet I'll never erase

for every dream I have I wish to see you there
I write to you to show my love and to show you that I care
so, with my love my sweet love I give to you tonight
to show my heart to show it true to show that there is light
and with my love with everything in me this letter I will send
in hopes that our love will never die, nor will it ever end

The Sun

What do you want from the sun so bright
think of 1 dream at night when the stars collide
with pride I stand to fight, and not hide
in the back of my mind there is a grand design
Blend in with the world like a jungle
be humble don't stumble grab that life before it crumbles
But what happens when danger turns to dust
you trust the person and that person breaks your love
and your heart bleeds tears and your pride dies within
So, what is more to find in the end
Disaster strikes the night in the dream you had of a star
of a light so real with a beautiful delicate star
it burns like fire, for thirst and desire
a tear away my reason to look up and climb higher
but I can't give up I cannot fall
to let it all slip, I cannot, not at all
what do you want from the sun with a light so bright
with the dream so true, it appears at night
when you close your eyes, and you venture away
fate from that night to see a sunny day

Someone

If they could only see what I can see
something beautiful and also sweet
you grew one day in a garden of life
And stole my heart complete

why must you suffer with the beauty so stunning
if anything, to gain it would be you I'm wanting
inside your eyes are stars of light
and in your heart, I will be tonight

Without You

If I could be without you my life would slowly fade
Nothing to love or live for, you're gone so far away
This shadow haunts me, and you're nowhere near
Without you there is no light but only fear
I'm lost without you and lying here to linger alone
If I could be without my love, I'd have no home
This bed I lay upon with one half gone
To lay here without you, I cannot go on
My sun, my day, my light of love is dead
I cannot fade, I must not die but I will live instead

Salem Heart

I do not feel what was felt in the rain
we walked for miles in the Virginia valley
With sullen eyes she killed my pain
That is why I want her badly
she's gone from me, and I shine no more
and then my soul bears a sore
and then my heart bears a stain
this is the hurt which brought back pain
I do not feel what was felt before
so, with the heart of war this blood will pour

What My Eyes Do See

I see your smile and you blush of a red
to feel your lips a kiss instead
I see your eyes and you're shy to stare

to look away I would not dare
I see your skin and to fill it there
I touch the heart because I care

An Undying Love
you are what I say and more
I've never seen a woman so beautiful before
you are the words that I write
To see you it would be tonight
you are what is wanted from my heart and mind
what was being wanted is no longer hard to find
you are here in front of me and my sight is clear
no longer distant from me my love for you is near
a hand to hold and I will hold you tight
I'll do it today and especially tonight
feel my warmth to caress your skin
not only the outside but also within
I am the son, and you are my moon
darkness is scattered when it's just us two
Close your eyes and imagine my kiss
upon your lips from my lips to kiss
to kiss your skin and to feel your hair
I'd grab you gently so that you will care
you are the fairest more beautiful than Paris
you are what is written it is my heart that is being given
we are on a cloud just you and I
a place so high, higher than this Sky
we are in heaven a place where you were born
my dearest sweet Angel without you I am torn
in those eyes I see a world
me as your man and you asked my girl
The times we've shared with the heart not broken
for it will never break because my heart has spoken

My Dear Distant Love

My dear sweet love, never let this affair fade
Oh, my evil love, you sure have a cold-hearted way
My dear darling girl, you take my breath some place
A place in heaven where God made your face
A face so sweet so pure which made me complete
You're the heart I have which causes mine to beat
You're my water, so cool and soft of feet
If only the distance closed in, our lips would finally meet

Do You Think About Me

I wonder what you're doing
If not me then what have you chosen
What else are you choosing?
You walked away with my arms wide open
I wonder where you're going
To search for you I could never do
It is my heart that I'm exposing
With pieces missing I'm torn in two
What are you thinking about
If it is not me then who's taken it all
Why become North when I am South
When I think about you, tears continue to fall
On a Wednesday it happened, wishing that you and I could be
With he thought of you only, do you ever think about me

Everlasting Love

You are my flower of light in a dark garden filled of night
Without a thistle or a thorn, your existence is why I was born
If roots be in heaven, then we will grow, in summer fields of a warm winter snow
Our case the color of your desire, and pierce the heart with all my fire
Your tears of rain will fall down on me to taste the water, I will drown with thee
a thirst for this sweetness and I taste and Ocean's tongue

I love you more and no less, and on this night your flower has come
it fills this garden with pleasure, my body is shaken buy your flower
this moment I'll always forever treasure, with no more tears to drown what
is ours

My Pure Love

you are my marshmallow so soft and when heated you melt in my mouth
with love
you are my milk so cool and when poured you soothed my tongue of white
a chill of milk you love me, and you are my snow so pure
and when felt deep within my soul you remain the reason my love will endure

Night and Day

I am in a night sky, starstruck
only bright line of all the earth
and I kill what darkness has trust
to gain my light in its worth
Glow in you my dear heart of love
more than stars and now the sun
your heart is what I have struck
and love is what made us one

In Your Heart

Tearing away from this piece of paper, it kills my disease of writing to you
but I must continue thinking of what to say, to give your shore the break of
day
the air is clear, and I am sure, but I cannot tell
for I am lost within the walls of a dangerous life
to touch your heart is to feel your skin
the paradise I've been searching for since then
and ever since I was struck by so by a love so sweet
I persist for your heart because it holds my beat

My December

You're like December, you are my time of the year
you are as cold as the winter, you are the sons only fear
December is in you, a year I had before
a winter which came true, a fear I will fear no more
for you possess the ice and the snow and the slush to keep me in
a winter storm is in you, but I possess a fire within
I will come for you in the month of May and my flowers will bloom on
your soul
my dear December do not fade away, remain with me to keep me whole

Take Away

Take away my food and the air that I breathe
Take away my clothes and also my water
Take away my treasures if there be any
But do not take the love I have for your daughter
We be but one heart, a beat of the ocean
Do not take from me what made me whole
Take from me, my hands or my feet
But do not take away what has made me sweet
The bitter taste of my past, she has set me free
This love is in one heart "please let it be"

Damaris

The dark twinkle in your eye, I embrace that sight of black
A star is pure to fill the sky, this love I give will never lack
Those cherries, your lips, I kiss; I feel upon that cloud of pink
This pleasure to stare I will not miss, and with my eyes I will not blink
A glimpse, I stare into shadows silk, I feel upon the many strands
Your hair is felt like coolness of milk, and skin of tan to compare to sand
With words of song you fill my ear, to fill my heart you let me see
A sight so sweet, you will appear, this beauty of you will always be

Pleasure

So wet, so tender, so moist are your kisses
So pure, so pleasant, so satisfying are your lips
To taste, to touch, to satisfy your mouth
I'd do with my chocolate, right here, right now
I'd feel your skin to make you quiver
As cold as winter I will make you shiver
I'd touch you there, your heart would be felt
Look at me and I'll stare to make your body melt
With skin like milk, I'd drink it all up
From the cylinder of this glass to the bottom of the cup
As beautiful as you are, angels do not compare
If your heart wants pleasure, I will please it there
To take your breath away will be something new
With sweet words of chocolate, the taste will be true
Skin felt deep to cause your mouth to open
Your skin, now heated, from what was felt frozen
This taste you have been given will continue to spread
To places in this pleasure other than in your bed

There is Love

There is life in your face and love in your eyes
Your smile is the joy to the ones who cry
Your tears are words I have never heard
But to hear you tonight, I'd kiss you instead
I would hold you tonight in my arms and in my bed
There is beauty in your heart a place I want to be
to create something new and to feel something sweet
I write to an angel who is beautiful and true
To write to another is something I could never do
There is love in this note and sincerity within
I write with my heart, to you my dear friend
To a girl so pretty so beautiful and sweet
I write for you tonight, allowing my love to leak

We Are Love

Fear me for I am he, I am the sky and the land
Fear me for I am you and we are the creation of man
The sky and the land I am creation of man we are
From break of day with the sun and sky
And we are like a midnight star
Fear me, for I am love, you smile with tears on belief
Take this heart I give to move, and in this life, you find relief
God is love above all you see, and we are his children and creation
We are life and love together, and God will love us all forever

My True Color

Feet of fall, my leaves have fallen
born of green to grow with you
Summer has passed to show what is true
And we are all that is left of pollen

We of Color

What is black and white and red all over
It is the world we must uncover.
You and I are now sisters and brothers
With black and white and more to discover
With red we cry and mourn our loss
And open the gates for a new birth
Let the children play with sticks and cloths
For they are the red, the new on earth
Are you the pure and I am death
We are bothered to put to rest
I am the light and night is here
You are the setting of the sun to appear
Let them play and play they must
What is a color if it is not us

The Path of light

You see the woods are black yet you go
Your feet tread this path of the weak
With warning of wolves and howls they blow
You walk continuously into the deep
Lost in fear and in search of morning
You wait but you walk, hoping for light
You fall and cry and tears are pouring
And woods of black have held you tight
Warm thoughts you feel from what's been told
You were taught that love will never harm
On bended knee your faith unfolds
And on your shoulder will lay his arm
And suddenly Ishtar of love has come
To guide your feet to a place you belong

The Sight of Love

this is my life I love and on a paper I write
I see the heart in a woman despite the fight
still on my mind when seconds have passed
I have finally found you yes you at last
I think of the clouds, the one we are sharing
now I dream of you with soft the love comparing
I found you on a night so lonely and cold
That dark dream vanished when I opened my soul
My heart is directed in your life and in your eyes
One day you will be, only you, in my skies

Strength in Shadow

There is a shadow buried in the cold wet dirt
the void of silence which slips in tears
it travels deep within all of the earth
and conquers victory to create our fears

death is dwelling among those who live
why waste a life which was created new
why take away when he wants to give
to hide in shadows, you cannot do
rise to love and remember your heart
a joyous thing so warm and pure
to live in love is his greatest art stand with me and together we'll endure

Do Not Betray Me

Do not plot a plan against the stone
With feathers you come up will not own
For I am great
Do not leave me lying there
Pick me up if you care
For I am great
Do not swear or hurt or kill this love
Why hate what I share, why must you shove
For I am great
I am the stone, and you are my feather
Opposite of dreams but we need each other
For we are great

Drained

To sink so low, you drop below my feet
Drained and sunken in mud you crawl
Scattered and spilled to spoil the weak
Born of roots and graves to your fall
Forget the sun and the moon, and light in the sky
It's faded far away to stay and to please
The memory of laughter has frowned so dry
And this grave is ours, a place which sets us free

My Lonely Cry

My lonely night, so quiet and filled with grass
With trees, this meadow has my heart at last
This place is of silence and shadows and of clouds
Rain and tears to cause a soul to drown
I'm stuck and alone in darkness without you
Alone and covered n paint made blue
To lie here beneath the dream of love I dry
I float away in tears of pain to close my eyes and die

Craving You

Your warmth I lust for more
I think of you day and night
To taste your lips, to kiss the core
I lay my hands on your thigh
To run my hands along your breasts
The nipple has stood to be kissed as well
To fill your flower and all the rest
I'd do what lustful things can tell
I want your heart, your neck and this lust
I crave this love with heat and with passionate trust

Careless Things

Cornbread cookies, caramel cakes
Cream pies, coffee, candy we ate
Chicken chocolates, and cheddar cheese
Chips or corn, the kind of cream
Carrots, clams, with calories built
To wash it all down you will need milk
We drink, we eat of careless things
To fill in the void of a fairy tales dream

Life

And at awn we wake to sleep
To fill our heads of a dream
What fun do we have without a plot
If only we could be whatever we're not
My sky is grey one day of winter
Life is as cold as a day in December
But suddenly the light of sound I hear
If only I could be anything and everything
This world would spin around my sleep
But I wake and I arise from this dream
If only I could remain in closed eyes so deep

This Sound

Of rage and horror and in the sky there you are
This sound of love and thunder bolts strikes the fallen star
I hear hat rock you cast into the earth's core
Of danger and terror but I will hear no more
Do run and flee, fly far from this sound
It has struck me before and I fell to the ground
The feeling of love and of the sound you fear
Listen to my echo, it is my voice that you will hear

Together Forever

Together again we be, you and I together forever
Forever with love in my hand, my life and love be sweet
My life, my world, you are to me
Together you and I will be
Forever together you and I, together forever we be
My love for you is so alive, I'll cherish it for eternity

Blinded

I am lost in a tunnel
It is confusing to me
To crawl in darkness
I am blind, can't you see
I am cornered by blackness
It is haunting me so
To crawl in the darkness
I am blind without a glow
And lost in your heart
Why torture me there
Please shed a tear for me,
For pain has struck me without a care

Drink of Life

There was once upon a time, a drink of cherries mixed with lime
A juice of life I quenched upon, and now that juice is all but gone
I sipped this drink until an ocean gathered
Dry land disappeared to be covered more faster
Of cherries and lime my mouth is full
Once upon a time when my cup was pulled

I Paint

In this rainbow I color, I paint, I am
I stand as brown in color and paint for I am
In this rainbow, I create life
Are you me or are you white?
We are dark, or we are light
But I see color and I paint my life
In this rainbow here I stand
Here I paint, and here I am

Follow Your Heart

Follow the beauty you see right now
If only your feet knew the steps, how
How to follow something so beautiful and so rare
It is a miracle for her to know you are there
Walk up on this lady and give her your words
Deliver, and it will be rewarded now you are hers
So, do not be afraid to capture your dream
Because your love of life is not as far as it may seem
Follow your heart and getting your life
Your feet will know which one is right

Light of Life

In this dark deed I bare a light
Some see me and spit but not upon my sun
Stare at my love and endure pleasure
For my sky is filled with endless light
Charge at love and kiss its embrace
In a garden of Eden my life is born
So soft are the grass and pedals to measure
And in this love, I see your smile
What does it mean to dream of little?
Low living in the country and we climbs end
And on trees we stand to gaze upon that light
Leaves are falling but I remain
I embrace gravity with love of the land
With this heart and my hand, I write
I cherish every word and smile, I love this sight, this beautiful light

A Fighting Heart in the Dark

I feel my fingers fading and ink decreasing
It is slowly disappearing and fast of freezing
No thought of this or emotion, just letters

No coats for this winter, nor jacket or sweaters
I feel no numbness, no feeling, only oblivion
It is slowly going away, no life, minus a billion
Minus love, minus hate, nothing can be compared
I am in a void and darkness and lost in air
Do you see me smile, yes, I fight
Giving up is a trait my bark will not bite
I fight no matter if in darkness or light
I fight because giving up is never right
So, I charge at the darkness, and the void and oblivion
To one day see the light, and love of stars plus a billion

A Dream Come True

Her smiles I swear is sparkles in water
In love I used to be, I look no further.
I am her hair, long and smooth
And in discussion is our loves move
She is my body, hard and firm
Dark-milked skin taste to learn
We seek love and I am lost
In her eyes my vision never costs
In my heart and my mind
She is my love, the dream I will find
I wake to search, to seek my half
To find my place in her arms at last

Trapped

My heart is in knots, and you are the string
My love, why do I have hate inside of me
It is pleasure to hurt your heart to rust
And throw your tears to dry in dust
Your smile and joy were my bright of hills
And song of music to my ears to hear
Your voice so warm to keep me covered

And in winter I'm coated because of you
But now I tremble and resist to love
I blink my heart and push and shove
I cannot cry a thunderstorm as you do
My weather is summer with water of few
And you stare at me so why would you care
My heart are pieces of the memories we will always share
Fear to love so letting go is definitely a must
I leave your sweet song because of a lack of forever trust
I dread the years of my future alone
But my heart is in the knots of home
I'm tangled and mangled and trapped inside
And while you sleep soundly, in secret I write

Why Lie

The things that I leave behind, replays a voice in my mind
Of the rules we followed, and the heartless dream swallowed
Didn't want to go but tears fall, the days spread my shore to trust nobody at all
So far away from the love that I felt, with words so deep in a letter to make
my lover's heart melt
They told me forever it forever is a lie, So I fly alone in a dark grey sky
I fly away, so far from the truth, from old days of hurt and pain to new
days of youth
I am far away, away from you, I never wanted to leave, so why not tell the truth

My Back

My back, scratched and scarred for life
My back, you turned on me, why
Why hurt my skin or cause so much pain
Now permanently placed is a continuous stain
You waited until the time was right
To peel the skin so deep that night
You dug into earth's ground to make me cry
Why, why did you choose my back that night

Kill my stare and enlighten me with pleasure
And steal my brown color with a scratch to measure
My back, scratched and scarred for the rest of my life
My back, the place where you hurt me that night

Dead

You took my heaven and made me hell
Cast me into the center of a spell
I dwell in your hate and in fear I lay
I perform lies and disguise myself to pray
You too me in your heart to burn my soul
I died that day on a day so cold
I'd dead and no longer here to roam
Where are you evil beauty, I want to go home
I'm alone; tears l constantly in this land
Of hate I stood, of love I stand
Never again will I cry to you my dear hate
I will walk away into the deep and past hells gate

Bonita

My beautiful love, my bonita, my life
My señorita today and especially tonight
My bonita, so far so pure, so sweet
My love, my life, my puzzle is complete
My tear, my cry, my pain, my world
My dear, my light, my pain lives no more
My heart, my joy, my beautiful Nikita
My life, my love, my beautiful bonita

Cuts

Scrapes and cuts, deep wounds; I can't heal
I am not whole; my soul will never feel
That scar, my scrape, these permanent cuts

I am paced into thorns and constantly rushed
Since birth I felt hurt and pain
Drenched in blood and dipped in stain
I will never be whole again

Discovery of Love

I found you, didn't I
I found the essence of smells from a garden
I found you in that place
I found you in the sky. I dream of stars looking into my eyes
I dream of flowers to bloom in May. I dream of that day
I dream of that sight. I love your eyes
I love your hair. I love your smile
I love your stare. I found this place
I found you
I found love forever
Hoping this love will endure

Cats and Dogs

Scratching, nagging, fighting, biting
Screeching, burning, meowing and clawing
Cats and dogs we be of this world
And curiosity of both has killed the girl

Soft soft Sound

Blowing without a sound
A hollow whisper in the ground
I stare at its presence
As it constantly frown
I am here to hear your call
You call upon me from the fall
Leaves blow low and calm to my ear
And past the other to blow away fear
Love feels so good from what

I'm so glad he's mine
A soft sweet sound that I hear
A love so pure, I'll never die

To Build Your Body

Roses are fed with waters so blue
Like blades of grass, they grow when in dew
For petals they make and beauty they create, and smells are new
When thy roses are in bloom

Do You Care

I care I swear
Do you even care
I care I swear
Do you care at all
I fall for you
Do you even care
I crawl to you
Do you care to look
To see my efforts wanting you
Do you care of what I do
I care I swear
But do you even care
To compare this love, ours is poor
But do you even care
This love is no more
Because you do not care
I cared; I swear

Love Shown

Warm heart and cheeks to cherish forever
Cool breeze to breath from your mouth
Like the shores and Andy beaches on your skin

Sung gold strands to compare to your hair
Tall green grass to grow like your legs
Spring waters to be shampooed with our flower
And in May you bloom so precious and beautiful
The many colors your eyes have changed
To fascinate my smile and the joy it brings
Never chill like winter to show no love
Do not freeze like December to blow me and shove
Lean your every burden on my heart to ache
And your beat will remain there for your save
Your jewel is too precious too pure to leave
If winter in December comes, I will be your sleeves
Soft plum lips to taste and kiss upon forever
That cool breeze which blows from your mouth
When we kiss, I feel upon your sandy shores
No more escape from this love, you're perfect
I'm perfect for you; accept me my love
Our love will last, to show my love, my life I'll prove

Heaven

Here are those lives I want to see
Of ghost, and love and hypocrisy
And drifts of wood with was once a ship
I dare not acre because I was meant to skip
I am not here to say when or where
Or the very reason of devils because they do not care
But I tear my page; I constantly cry
I dream of a land and place so high
I cry a tear of rain drops to see
But that place is for you and me
A place of love and safe haven to exist
I can't wait to see such a place; a place like this

Life Alone

Cold and dark in this love
I have no one I can trust
This love has come to hurt
To hate me for such dirt
For no worth, I am alone
This life I live, I live on my own

One Life

My life is filled with the days that grow
Whether rain, sleet, hail, or snow
My life will always be here to show
How I fill about his life I live
Or the many presents of roses I give
As long as you are here to care
I will always be there, I swear

Permanent Lust for Love

I crave this sex
This kiss for women
My hands to ones chest
I lust this lover
This heart of cotton
I crave the heat of passion which is left to cover
I embrace it all
This intercourse of love
I enter into life, to love, install
I sincerely love you
This drug of love
To lust permanently, I will always do

Last Time

I am done being me
Please set me free
I and done with lies
Please let me fly
I am done being me
I am now free
I am writing for the last time
This will be my last line
I am done

Learn to Love

Listen to it beat and learn to love
Touch my soul and speak thereof
Caress the mind and multiply life
Learn to love and do what's right
Peace t heart and joy of song
To sing of happiness and do no wrong
Lay down Lillie's where your lips will kiss
And paint me pictures of love to exist
Then sound me a song for this heart to beat
To play me a tune of something sweet
To listen to it beat; I learn to love
I have been given life to speak thereof

Dream

Close your windows or there are nightmares
Slow your slice for mouths do swear
Cherish dreams which do come true
Believe in them for they believe in you
Children sleep with eyes of innocence
And it is us who search like there's no end to it
Why stress what is grown when dreams are here

We of adults have so much to fear
Close your hate and open our hearts
And there is where you'll find a start
Open your love and feel what's real
For dreams are the things we must heal

Hurt

I remember her name
Just as the same T was just a name
She made it rain
I remember the pain
Just as the same
It was only pain
Which left stain

The Sky

There is blue, red, orange, and colors
And silhouette of symbols for our others
The wind blows them into a mix
To drown the colors in a bled to fix
It scatters the oils while surrounding the page
My colors are new with a sky left to age
light shined the sky to change the scene
To write upon this page so you know what it means
The color is pictured by what is shown
To be gifted with sky so we are all known

My Señorita Doreen

I did not see her until I heard her speak
A voice so soft the wind could not compare
But in my heart, I felt our words meet
And in an imported thought she was there
A beauty; sweet beauty, brown beauty, and fare

If only she was with me. If only I was there
A señorita Doreen my love, my dream
If only I was there, would you be with me

His Eyes of Sleep

His eyes are open to see your stare
His eyes are awake to show you a pare
His eyes are double to see the truth
his eyes are reflections to view what's in you
His eyes of sleep are tired from the day
His eyes re the eyes who made me in May
His eyes never tire, his eyes are heaven
His eyes are day 7 of sleep and rest
His eyes which are oven, so receive them, nothing less

The Zoo

Kids in the zoo
To find giraffes and bears
Off the jungle
And there, we find monkeys with no hair
Deep into the cave
Where bats stay awake
And not dump down under
We find ourselves a big earthquake
Kids in the zoo
Panthers and baloo
Bunnies and rabbits
This adventure is an artistic habit
Of eagles so bald and cheetahs who cheat
Yes, run so rapid with their spotted feet
So far, so deep, so much to see
Kids in the zoo
Just wait and you'll see

April 5th

All of the while she wanted a smile
She wanted a beginning, a newborn child
All the while, she cried, in hunger
And in this world, it pulls us under
Searching for love but darkness appears
And in this hole the black is near
Into oblivion, a void of hate
But all she ever wanted was a babe
One message left to find a way out
Sour towards the surface to see what it's about
Precious Gods light, love and happiness we see
A beautiful newborn child with a beautiful heart beat

Confession

I loved you all my life
My joy and comfort
Through days and years
All this love is what it's worth
True beginning for smiles and laughs
And after so much pain
My dear love, I've found you at last

No More Pain

To sleep forever, for eternity
I feel no pain, I remember me
Why do you cry when I am dead

Pure Beauty True Love

Volcanic eyes, to erupt would kill
But life in her should definitely heal

Her white day smile and night light sparkle
Will fill your heart more than anything partial
She dances with wings and twirls the wind
To feel her hurt is to dig deep within
Her silky-smooth hair will tell you dreams
Of a dark forest of Lillie's and roses in the spring
With a face of joy and smile of peace
I search to find no other, because my love is here with me

Doctor

Broken dreams have caused a nightmares
Without a flow of blood in my veins
Torcher my nights with aches and pains
To capture my tears down a flight of stairs
High fever, and a thought of you to cause it all
Hurt inside f my heart to bring a sudden fall
And cast me in bed to sit there
Without flow of love for me to tear
Legs like needles, so sharp and thin
And summer days gone to kill my peace within
Life is sweet to heal what has been offered
To kill this hate by the love of a doctor

Joker

Juggle your jokes with lies and lilies
Circle the truth with everything pretty
Clumsy acts concerning a laugh
To juggle your words to count the math
With colors of three to toss in the air
And fall on a canvas to cause a stare
You joke and play and make your money
But do not know what's really funny
So, laugh and lead your falls with play

And be the joke of every day
A joke you are, a joke you stay
A joke you'll be until the day you lay

Not Too Old To Heal

Broken limbs on the ground yet leaves begin to fall
From heaven's branches they came to call
In the depths of tears, the rain grows roots
Until one day that the sky calls for you
Shadows come under the tree
But after the darkness the sun will be

Come Back to Me

In the torment of hollow torcher
I lean in for more o bury scorcher
Hot in the lots of a seasoned suns
To gain many browns of tans and tons
In paradise, the time for treasure
I lean in for more to only pleasure
Wonders and wishes to come true for us
In torment of hollow torcher, I find love

Death of darkness

Silence in the night has killed my life
Secrets kept underneath to hide the truth
Eyes of hurt will stain this light
And lips kept closed to control our youth
Weakness has blown into seasons so warm
To cause much evil and to cause more harm
The question of why has crossed your mind
And in your heart this love is blind
Leave the lost or heal the hurt
From laid back leaves of seasons so cold

And in the bottom, there lays the dirt
Of a sin so wrong from days of old
Keep your youth and live for the light
Dark deeds appear to kill your life
An angel I am because of death
And you may feel you have no breath
But hold this life and feel no pain
No hurt will overcome when light is here
And in this love our love comes again
So, kill this wrong so there is no more fear
A secret kept underneath to hide the truth
Has taken my life and destroyed my youth
Dark deeds are among you, but my light is here
So, do not be afraid and do not have fear
I am your angel, a lost sheep who came home
Silence while you sleep for the darkness is truly gone

Beautiful Fairy

In these wings I bring you flowers
To the end of time, I still have power
I tickle your heart to bring more dust
And in this beauty, there is only trust
The steps you take are shown in the sky
And everyone seeks to know the real reason why
I see the eyes of green and blue and purity
If only it'd be me that is inside this jewelry
Nags and sparkles and things to carry
I think of you only, my beautiful fairy

Dead Branch on a Tree

Alive or alone we shake of death
With a wrist to twist and bend
Killing the sun without a friend
Where demons are to put to rest

The Sky

In dark times with lightning and thunder
He night will cover to put us under
In the lightest moment it shines with so many smiles
And in that star, they travel for miles
Snowballs will fall to cover the ground
And rain will come so look around
Worth hail and sleet and everything slippery
We see it a fall like drops of shivery
So bright so straight the sun will come
But the night be the end of the story of me

Hell

I give in to the evil and plans to plot my dreams to fail
And in this world hate exists and continues to prevail
Why silly things of baffle continue to strong you
And in the light of night the darkness haunts you
I am alone and in death of breath to fail
And in the darkness of it all my energy prevails

Dead

Carnal thoughts of my stupid mind
Will tear my heart f broken lies
Conjure this hell so my eyes be closed
And in return I bury the soul

Raindrops From My Heart

I felt it fall down on my chest
And the rest would say it was you
Turn in truth it was a smile
Something I haven't felt in while
The cool wet feeling of life

Soft joy I would reveal every night
And in the day, you fell too
He day of a dream to come true
To reveal that one hope of love
I reveal to you my raindrop from above

Shadow In My Eyes

I see brown in my mirror, The image buries me deep
A familiar way of being cloned, From forms of my head to feet
I vision this brown splashed with mud, compared the same to paint my art
And in this work, I stare once more, to see this shadow washed on the shore

On this Night

On this night I write to you
The sleep you are in is very deep
But I stare at your nightmare
I enter your dream to fight off the pain
The monster I was I am no more
I am your drop of rain
The fire you felt will burn no more
I am your feeling felt true in a letter
The everything you've always wanted forever
On this night you sleep away very deep
A wonderful dream of you and I
Tonight, I write of a love so sweet
A love so endless it will never die

Life of Mine

There is a cave I entered yesterday, and today I have found another
I go about my way in pieces, to find out why we need each other
Two caves and one boy, which do I choose?
I close my eyes and guess it then, and open them to upcoming news
But which is the destination I need to find, to better my future of something kind

One is long and the other is short, but neither is easy to pick or sort
The long one is dark and cold, he short one is as white as old
With the short so bright to my eyes, the long cave is full of flies
But a challenge I must take, to further give my safety away
A risk I take to pursue adventure, I enter the cave where there are no answers
A cave so confusing yet exciting to take, I enter the labyrinth for years to stay

I'll Never Be

I'll never be what I used to be, I'll never be me
The legs and arms shackled in chains, will never set free
I'll never be the light of love or center of a care
I'll never be what faith has felt, because it was never there
I'll never heal from years ago, nor present or future griefs
I'll never heal from hurt so permanent because of false beliefs
I'll never be perfect, Prince Charming, nor a king from crop to cream
I'll never be the happy joy, but a boy of a love, I'll never be

Honorable Henry

Always on time for the wood to be split
Ole honorable Henry, the boy who was six
In a hurry for school, to give an assist
Honorable Henry, going through the list
Ready for the bus, to go home and play
Ole honorable Henry, the boy who could say
"Comment allez vous?" Or "How do you do?"
Ole honorable Henry, the boy we all knew
But one foggy day when walking on the road
Ole honorable Henry bent down to grab a toad
Not knowing traffic coming, not knowing about the truck
Ole honorable Henry got pinned and jammed and also stuck
The Doc shook his head and fell to the floor
For the boy who was six has entered heavens doors
The pain that we felt will never be swept away
For ole honorable Henry is gone but continues to play

The Wall of Ants

Putting my head against the wall
I could not see at all
I fell to my knees and instantly felt
A stinging desire of an itch when knelt
With plates and forks and food we ate
But not knowing of the red
A bite which bit me on that day
By claws upon its head
A viscous bite, an itch so fierce
It made me scratch and dance
The bite which bit me on that day
Was the bite of a big fat ant

The Path

When in the mountain I saw the crack
And down below he broke his back
For curve and slant and slope he went
And continued on until is back was bent
When back was back he headed on
Til time was old for the rise of dawn

I Think of You

Constant, brief breaths that I breathe, I persist to write
For my mind is easy to perceive and yet I might
Be of life I think, and open to my heart, for you are there
I tear this reason apart to view beauty, and yet I care
For constant thoughts continue to fly and there you are
So much memory and joy you've given my eyes
Even though you remain far,
But my dear love, I think of you.

The Ride of My Life

At that moment I could not breathe
She was so beautiful in my sight, I gasped
I blink my eyes twice and fell to my knees
An instant pleasure has come at last
Her eyes of ember her lips of treasure
To lay me down and give me pleasure

Someone Special

Why give me money, when honey is sweeter
For your kisses fill my tummy, oh how I love your feature
And when you stare my way, I come towards you
For you create my everyday
And being your pen is what I will do
For you are my paper, and I am your writer
And we share our story to the universe
Oh, how I love this curse

Selfless

Where waters are blue, and sands are white
And grass so green where the love is true
And for one small line, and for this new view
Where water is the wine and the heart of yours is mine
And the heavens touch my skin
Where chills from a breeze blow
And in this love is life and you, I call my wife

Paranormal Trip

Picking peppers per pound plus peels
Parking Perry's plurals purposefully patting pills
To taunt the texture taking time to tick
Til the time taken takes time to trick

Per pound patty picked peppers packing pieces
Patting Perry's plurals piercing patterns per pepper
To train through the taunting to tear their trip
Taken until the time to terrorize this trick

Down by The River Side

Down by the river side where the kids would play
All but two by the riverside would play
The rocks would fly, the water would splash
The fish would jump, the kids would laugh
Shadows cover the light which sits on the waters
Hearing them playing, our sons and daughters

I Dwell in Hell

The window was open for you to come inside
My presence was made but you chose to hide
Why create a wall between our hearts
What made you drown the ship from the ark
I felt you in my dreams, to scream loves name
But you fade away into another day, opposite of the same
You burned my existence when you left
I crawl into a hole, second book on the shelf
I fade away as well, I dwell in hell

One More Day

I see you; I feel you; my house is filled with pain
I fell you; I see you; it remains all the same
Do not slither into my life and don my greed
For the reason is the season, and the thought is the need
The seed I bear, the hurt I wear; I tear away
Into a better love, up above into a new day

No Fools Allowed

I wrote a rhyme in school. I told you I was fooled
I rose from the bottom to pull the top to the roof
I rose, I flew, I dream of you
I will not be schooled
I will not be fooled

My Globe

Where is my father, where is my mother
When I was young, I had no brother
I had no siblings; I had no friends
I created hate, with the help of a pen
I wrote down the page and up the mountain
I did not stop until I finally found them
I opened my eyes and realized you
What did I terrorize when I met you
Pain, hurt deep, no heart, no soul
But love always exists and it made me whole
To fold, to flip, to flop I forgot
But I continue to write, my story is chopped

Love Me

I was a told story by one man: me
No soul knew my name; be
Be who you feel, feel who you are
I am not a zero. I am a star
Love is my name; God is my father
I will not have a dad, but I love my mother
Stay true to your thoughts and love all
I am the season created in the fall
My name is life, alliances forever
Love me dearly, love me my lover

I Wrote About You

My dad was alive, but he is dead
He is in my thoughts daily; he is in my head
Laced on my shoes, he lists every rap I stole
He stole my whole life and new I write
I write about love, hate, pain, no life
I write to write about life, no loss, no strife
Just life, just hate. No late note, I wrote

Pistol

Do not stop the game
Be the best that you want to be and no less
Focus on your journey and put your mind to the test
There are no limits to what you can do
You must always believe in you
Stay the course and finish what you start
Give it your all, especially your heart
Remember what was said, and live what was taught
For the love of the game, for love cannot be bought
Love is an art which we practice on the court
Work hard to be the best, no matter what sport
Live what was taught and love life forever
Be like the Pistol and never say never

In Class I Could Rap

I remember the days when I would spit a rhyme
I'd clap a rap for days and remember every line
I remember long ago when my teacher had to teach
And then I had to stand just to do a speech
I remember all the girls would clap when I would rap
My homeboys would applaud; I remember they'd give me dap
In class I would rhyme and at first it was for fun
But now that I'm a pistol, I have to draw the gun

I have to write my life, my story and more
I must show the world who I'm doing this for
And so, you will see, this light inside of me
The love of the rhymes for each line will always be

My Virginia Sky

My Virginia sky, Goodbye
My Virginia dream, I scream
My forever farewell, I leave
My Virginia girl, my Rachel Renee
I will always love you, every day

Free

Free is what you made me
Free is what I'll be
From under a rock to the top of a tree
I remain unchanged. I remain free

The Path That I Must Take

The road not yet taken nor broken by teeth
I chip away the pieces beyond my belief
This path of life we walk will tear down our wall
I will not close my ear to not hear the call
You see the tears of innocent eyes, heal them
Do not walk away from those sky's, reveal them

All the Same

Into your eyes I have grown fruit and land
I inherit this life; the skies begin to plan
My tongue pierced with truth, with total loss
Of hate, of greed, I do not pay the cost
I harness love and embrace pain

For we are not enemies, we are the same
This fruit which grew, this voice
Has risen among those of choice
I celebrate with song and write with love
I embrace joy, pain, and the heavens above

Out of My Head
We have grown apart for some time now
It has been das of anger and sadness
You sleep silently as I watch your sound
When will we both depart from such madness
I do not hesitate to play the fool, to urge our tears
You drown in them while you drool, it has been years
The hate, the level of no life, no love, no longing for lust
We hate, and despite what we hope to thrust there is not trust
I must be gone from you, for I do not know what to do
I have done so much dirt, but I hope we are both not through
I am out of this world and out of my mind
Out of my head, it's been some time

Deep into the Forrest Wood
Deep down into the forest I present by everlasting soul
I present my love on a platter; I present it whole
I taste the essence of lights and linen and set my sights on sounds
To rags we make the riches sweet

Once Upon a Night
Once upon a night when it was dark and cold
We walked through the woods with a drunken girl to hold
She swung to the left, she swung to the right
She didn't want to fall, so she held on tight
When we got to the party there was no more Bacardi
When we got to the spot, all of the girls were hot

Some were ugly, some were fine
Some were chubby, none were mine
I saw a girl dancing who was pretty as can be
I started moving towards her, hoping she'd dance with me
She looked like a flower, but no flower compares to this
When they start the countdown, I want a kiss
I turned my head for a moment, and she was nowhere in sight
While my friend was with a girl, I was looking for mine all night
Ten minutes later my friend said, "come on"
I looked for her one last time, but she was already gone
We went to the Waffle House to give a girl her purse
The whole night to me felt just like a curse
I thought I saw her in the car, but I didn't know
They asked me were we coming in and I said, "we have to go"
I texted the girl who likes my friend while staring at a star
"As long as you know that you're amazing then you are"
That what I texted her and I thought that was the end
But she texted me back and said I should call her friend
She said her name was Calli and she gave me her number
I looked through my yearbook and my eyes started to wander
I couldn't believe it, she's the pretty girl who can dance
So, I grabbed my phone and flew all the way to France
First class, on our way to a good conversation
Houston, we have a problem, but it was just the gravitation
We talked for a long time and landed on the Eiffel Tower
We talked for a long time, probably past an hour
I thanked the amazing pilot, whose name was Mallory
Once upon a night, when I met Calli

Lucy

In that moment I saw the ocean, for her eyes washed away the weary reasons
to become so blue. With the tint of red and mellow look of the sun, her hair
has covered every inch of perfume for it smells so strong, and yet I stood so
still to see the pleasure in her lips for they are moist and soft; if the sullenness
of her eyes could pierce through each heart, on paper I'd write about this

beauty, but she is more than the word we all adore, she is more, so much more. For you sweet Lucy I write tonight, to write to the hills upon your face and the mountains in your ear, place a word in that place for you hear me say that I adore thy lips, and thine eyes, and thy heart, and I adore the love that you have given me to write to thee. You are the earth, and also the heavens, for your beauty is paradise to my eyes, and your heart is the song which is the melody of love so tender and forever true.

The Diner at Denny's with You

Which had seemed like a dream was definitely true, for you are more than what it seems. Which kiss, these words, this dream, I'd give you more which I've created to fill me up. To give you this the cream, the sugar, and the cup; the words for my coffee to have cream. For you are day which has felt like a dream, has given me on your cheek will never stray. This reality of your eyes to gaze and turn away, for the blush words in this poem to be more complete. For summer is hot and my heart is the heat, for more reasons for this season to care. For expression, the joy in your stare, has given me so sweet, gave me a surprise. Your eyes, you're the words I've said I read your eyes, your lips, hoping your smile would somehow grow. With a fly on a window with wings to show, and me looking at you with skin as smooth as silk. With Drinking our coffee, with sugar and milk, me at the diner at Denny's with you. Which had seemed like a dream was very true, me at the diner at Denny's with you.

My Beautiful Shooting Star

A shooting star you are, but by far you are, so far you are my beautiful shooting star. Your eyes so pierced so direct and pure, this view of you I knew would endure. My lady, my dear, my love so far, so far you are my shooting star. I've missed you so, so long you've been gone, the moments have passed to this point in time, but now I write to you right now; my star, my day, my night, my dear, oh how I wish you were near. Id hold your body as I hold your heart, and do not shed a tear for we will never part. My lady, my dear, my love so far, so far you are my shooting star.

There is A Field in Your Face

Where white lilies and red roses grow
A heavenly paradise is that place
Wherein, pure and faithful falls the snow
You are like a summer day
You're more pretty than a morning in June, You're the reason flowers bloom
in May You're the glow that appears on the moon
Your voice is like a bird
A song recorded in my mind; I memorized every word I remember every line
I'm glad that he made you
As my lover and more
I never saw a more sweeter face
Then that I stood before

My Beautiful Flower

You have been planted to grow
But your colors you do not show
Because the weather is rainy and cold And in your fear you continue to fold
To lay in dirt to stay so safe
But dear sweet flower come from that place
For your beauty is rare and warm to the fire
So, show your color for another to admire The wind may blow, the rain
may come But for your beauty bares the everlasting sun And I am here my
dear to let you know That the roots of this love will always grow To show
you light, and care, and trust To show you that there's life for us
Because you are my beautiful flower

Comparing Thee

For every stare that we share will be a kiss to compare. For every kiss that
I wish to give to you, but I miss. For those lips I see are tender and moist
and, in that touch, I taste your voice.
To hear such a voice is to melt thereafter, with a pearl so pure no other would
matter. For you are my summer, my sweet rose in June. For every stare that

we share will be more to consume. For every hug that you give will devour the winter for spring to live. For warmth of life, I wish to show, and in this feeling our kiss will grow. Because the kiss that we share will be our love to compare.

In My Mind

In the middle of my mind I find this design, behind the view of you I find something true, and yes, it is beauty. Your world filled with skies and hills and plains, plateaus and planes, rivers and oceans and also the most devastating explosions and yet, only there do I see the reason to stay furthermore, thy beauty is the love that I treasure, and I look more to discover a sound, a word, thy voice is among a song no bird, no word, no sound so pure could I ever endure, but dear sweet love, I adore thy beauty, for you are the reason for my existence, the reason for my being, and the everlasting understanding of why I love thee every day.

Humble Bumble

Humble me you bumble bee
The bee up in the tree
The bee I see that bumble bee
The bee I'll always see
You humble bumble the bumble bee
The bee up in the tree
The bee I see, you bumble bee
The bee who flew to me

Chunky Monkey

That little boy that jolly babe
The stinky smell he gave
With a nose so full and cheeks so big
With eyes so wide you darling kid
My chunky child my heart and soul
My beautiful monkey, with love I hold love you monkey, the chunkiest of babes
The sticky little smell of which he gave

With my all I give and my all you are My chunky little monkey, my
shining star

Dreamer of Dreams

If that were me, I'd be obscene, but that dream is just a dream, if I were
you, I'd dearly use this chance of fame to be, to smile and laugh and
telegraph my heart from ground to air, and soar so high as never before,
if only I could care. If time were me and you were the tock id tick you off
your feet, but fairytale and caramels are as sweet as they can be, but if I
were thee, ole jolly me would love and laugh and live, the joys and dreams
of everything, but a dream is what I give.

Her Fruit

As beautiful as ever this lady she be, a woman named Lucy a beautiful tree,
and her fruits are sweet and juicy and ripe, I'd eat from her tree every day
and every night. Because she is juicy and also sweet, and my Amber, your
physique is why I eat. I taste that fruit I taste that juice; I taste the taste
you bare to give because your lips are sweet to me and because your limbs
are loose. And that is why I grab that fruit to taste that tender juice, to bite
into your fruit of love because those limbs are loose.

Golden Goddess

Flown in from a place of clouds, and like the sun which touches the waters,
it remains the touch of her lips I feel of moist and purity; with hair of silk
and skin of milk and eyes of webs the spiders spun and hands of claws but
soft to hold and in thy dress their be your breast and in those eyes thy sly
disguise, those slender thin eyes of skies, thy beautiful heart dear heart of
red, I slowly surrender this poem which is read.

A Bed of Rose

A bed of you, with the scent of love
A rose so red, for you my dove

A dream slept warm, of a red rose
A sleep so deep, for you I suppose Surrounded by petals, drowned in red
Crowded by you, the Rose of my bed
The splendid red flower of what life gives That splendid delicacy where my love lives The essence of elegant design of my heart That forever scent of nature made of art
A treasure kept in sheets of satin
A hope came true, knowing it would happen My Rose, my dear, my warm sweet flower
My joy so red, my food to devour My lady, my lass, my night and my day
My warm scent of love where my love will lay

Dinner for 2

If only one could be with the other but they are separate and apart without a lover
For 2 is lonely tonight and the one who is not present is one and out of sight. Two chairs two plates one dinner date at 8, but alone 2 will be, forever and for eternity.

To My Dear Heather

Dreaming of this lady has given my reality a woken embrace of life, for the illusion is the dream of her one day becoming my wife. But the tossing and turning of seeing her right before I wake, is the same reason I wish that the truth from this dream could not be fake. I am slowly remembering the mistake I made of not asking God to continue this dream, for I am alone when I wake, and I am missing my reason for being. You and only you are the reason I sleep, to dream of such beauty, to embrace your heartbeat, to devour your every presence with the kiss of my eyes, to remember this moment forever, hoping it'd never die.
Your beloved Henry

Writing about you

While you were sleeping, I was doing something persistent, writing about those lips and wanting tons of kisses. That intimate feeling felt in my mind and in my thoughts, made it that real, just to feel what was taught. Mind over matter and you'd be stuck on my mind, people say looks don't matter but dang girl you are fine. Like wine I sip that heart and like juice I drink you up, and if you were my beverage, no doubt I'd be that cup. You're my cranberry cherry with that extra spoon of sugar, if I take one more drink, I'm for sure going to put up with her. We stay talking from daybreak to night fall and chatting from sunup to sundown, and I still be up when you're asleep just to make sure you're the happiest in town

Tonight I write

In this moment I write to you, to you I write, I write tonight. Of a beauty so real, so natural to feel, so new to me, but a beauty you be. I treasure such heart, such life in your eyes, and in that sea, it lights up your skies. For days are light and nights are you, and so I write tonight, tonight I write to you.

She Told Me to Fly

She told me to fly
To venture forth without her air
She told me to soar away
But I did not dare
She forced this feeling away
This pain stuck and terrified me
With disbelief I could not stay
Because she was not happy
So, I fly, I soar as I've never done before I embrace this new air for, I breathe I love this embrace furthermore and that is why I have to leave
Because, she told me to fly

The Hidden Truth

There was a tree planted to hold deep
A secret kept from above and underneath
The root of the tree was already buried
So, a truth kept hidden would not be carried

Egg Salad

You're white like an egg salad, like the crushed pressure given by a mallet.
That pound that pushes that pressure persist, to give the smash of egg salad
a flick of the wrist. Egg salad, for the elders, so tasty to the tongue, so I peel
the eggs because my fingers are young. I peel, I place, I put them in salad. I
pound, with a push, to persist with my mallet. And that is the story of the
delicate egg salad.

Poison of Pain

She said goodbye with her eyes
She could not open her mouth
Her car was filled with poison
And in that payment came my tears
The fear of oblivion to my ears
The silence of her sweet words
And in that poison came the distance
I will never begin to recover
And with the distance there will be no other

Sweet Smile

At work you smile, At home you smile
On the phone you smile, On my cloud you rest
Your eyes are skies, Your hair of cherries
Mixed with golden love, and a heart of purity
Mixed with the above, for all that is in me

Happy Mother's Day

A mother of 4 and comes one more
A mother of mine so here's your line
A mother you be a mother you are
A mother so strong like a shining star
A mother among mothers who has given me

Four plus another and a mother you be
So, before I enclose this note to you
I'd like to propose a rose or two
For you dear mother among others you be
So, I write you a poem for you to see

Stuck on you

Roses are red, you're stuck in my head,
for Violet's so blue, I see only you.
The flower among many, a rose among few,
but if there'd be plenty, I'd still be stuck on you.

Beautiful Woman

As pure as white as light as night as bright as the star from a place so far,
that's what you are and what you are I like, because day is white, and
dark is night. Your feelings I feel your heart, it beats, of love and purity
and surely, you're sweet. For this feeling you feel and that heart which
beats will continue to be heard for the feeling is sweet. And you my dear,
my beautiful woman, a woman so special, a woman of tears, a woman
of laughter and joy to my ears. The feeling you have will spread to me,
because the feeling I feel will always be.

I Sit

I sit, and daytime sits with me I wait for you to come into my life
Night comes and I am alone
And I continue to be still until you are home
1 sit motionless and wanting you so
I wait but I do not know
Neither day nor night justifies this feeling
And so, I will sit here furthermore
Furthermore, for you, I will wait

Lilly

I creep into the water, into a wet spot of silence, but there I find my voice and I can no longer hide it; for I am caught. I must jump, I must hop away for I am Lilly. She has given me this name as if I am a flower, but a frog I be and am caught at this hour. Lilly I am and a frog I be, a mystery in your hand now set me free, for I am Lilly. I am green, I am brown, I am the color not yet found, so place me on the ground and let me be, for I am a frog, and she calls me Lilly.

Dear God,

Please take care of my brother
A man with more love and joy
A gift given like no other
And that is why my words deploy from mouth to ear and ear to heart
This heart held on to never part
To part from us to leave with you
Into a place that is so true
A place of life, love, and light So far away but forever bright
Dear lord, please lord, watch him sail to you For waves of waters can not undo
The sail set high which brought his soul
Forever gone to make us whole
To see you now, it makes me write About your love which came in sight
Beloved brother, my friend I see
What pain has surrendered to white flag thee
For no more pain, the retreat to love Has given you wings to fly far above
Above into heaven, and forever into paradise
A place so surreal and for real it is nice

Imagination

A place so surreal and for real it is nice You smile, they weep, you grin, they cry I smile with love to leak for angels are meant to fly
So, fly dear heart, dear spirit, dear words

The simple command of love that's barely ever heard
The many memories, the forever accounts Of the things that were done
will never amount To the things we'll do when I see you again
My mentor, my brother, like no other of a friend
Descend into life and enjoy paradise
Because it is surreal and for real it is nice and for you who do cry, for those
who shed a tear
Put a hand over your heart and there he will appear
Listen to hear it closely, the beat, his sound The voice of my brother, like
no other, he is found
For if you miss the kiss of a voice you used to hear
Place your hand over your heart and my brother shall appear

Be Mine

Be my baby and I be your man, be my lady and I hold your hand, take you
places you didn't know exist, be my baby forever and forever I be your kiss.
We take trips into London and vacations into Rome and spend the night
on Venus before we come back home.

Tonight, I Sing

I sing a tune of more than June
The day I come I come for you of beautiful lips and eyes to see I come for
you, I sing for thee Tonight I write, tonight I sing for my lady love, my
Billie B My forever girl, my lovely world I sing to thee, my darlin girl to
thee I sing, to thee I write To thee I sing, tonight I might

My Beautiful Lil Peanut

You have opened my skies to fill my eyes with complete life and with an endless
touch, a taste with tender care and love; I place no woman above you. And that
is why I write to your skies, to fill your eyes with what's worth looking into, to
see that joy you have brought to my life, that spark that I have been searching
for, but more you give and give even with just the thought of you gives me a
reason to write, to dream, to love you and only you.

A heart felt storm

pull it back and my heart burst with a pulse, with a startling discovery of a murder I once committed. the lightning strikes and thunder sounds which struck a mountains volt, and in that storm a whistle to hear, for the heart has made its pulse.

The grave

What if I existed in a grave
the cemetery of the living to die without age.
What if I were already dead,
alive in one world and the other I'm red.

The Ball

I put us in a ball where the links are of yarn and of chain with the same to commit what is bound
And as round as we see what we walk upon and lay
But in shadow beneath the ball, we will throw it all away
We will play and we will laugh of the laughter in the same, but the chain and the yarn will be torn from the rain
But in this land, we do see what we bury so deep, and in this ball we will fall all the way beneath our feet

Tasha

My dear, sweet as an orange, my friend, pure as light and day, my vanilla taste, for the tip of my tongue did devour you so, my beautiful flower, you spring in every month, a growth that will not end. What is that face of something sweet? So moist are your lips I taste that strawberry feeling, those lips so wet and wonderful, I could not resist them at all. And that stare you give so long and desirable, I did not flinch to see it, for to miss it would cause me to suffer. Those gorgeous eyes, I can't imagine anything as breath taking as the two things that We call stars, for your eyes are what I say: bright light in the night stars. And I persist to further write to you my darling beautiful friend for life. It is hard to find a friend like this and so a kiss I send to show it so. A kiss I wish I didn't let go; a kiss I dream of waters to flow, deep in my mind my dear friend you glow. Your body, your tender juicy edible body has given me a new way of looking at a woman, for your body is paradise to me. No, nothing is wrong.

Your Flowered body

Deep in my mind my dear friend you glow. Your body, your tender juicy edible body has given me a new way of looking at a woman, for your body is paradise to me. No, nothing is wrong with your warm sweet sensational body. It melted my hands when I felt upon its surface, and it heated my body and watered my lips. That is the most gifted body I've ever touched, with lips so perfect and eyes so genuine I have more to say, for the heart that you carry, it is the beat that keeps my hand wanting it so. My dear darling friend, your heart creates oceans to move and mountains to crack, and tides to rise, and for my words to continue. You must know how important and special you are. Time is moving, and I have only known you for less and seen you so few, but the little we know, this time is new, and this message is long but again, you must know, and you will know that what you have read should be expressed to you daily, what you have read is true; from me to the most beautiful woman in the world. Never forget that, always remember this, for this is yours to keep for as long as those irresistible eyes shall remain open.

A Night When She Became Mine

I flew to her that night and she took me to a world of paradise
I traveled in the air with her, and we created many clear skies
She became my night air, my forever moon so bright
And I became her sunny breeze within the trees that night
This feeling is felt with feathers of few to fly forever and forever with you
I write tonight about a girl I gave a love to create a new
And in that new which we have made I promise to always keep us close
For you are true, my one true girl, my moon so cool, my forever rose

Hope

How to come as one
On the demand of what we crave
Pour the love in a cup
Ending with life to equal our faith
From the fruit we drink the juice
And from the juice we fill our souls
And in hope we find the use
To come together as a whole

Lord of my Love

Lord of my love, Father of my faith
King of your kingdom, Lord of my love
the love from above, Lord, dear sweet lord
the light in my life, The sweetest word
Oh, father of my faith, King of your kingdom
I cherish this love, oh father, oh lord I love you
Oh King, dear sweet king, this song that I sing
My lord of this love, a love from above.

Take me there

Take me there, to a place where I can escape
Take me there, to a world of dreams and space
Take me, take me away
To a land of life and light
Take me away, to a house of mine despite
What has happened in that home
Take me there for I am alone

Sixteen years

And 15 has gone from me,
For days of the years, we can not pretend ,

And the weeks will tremble, Into months they bend
For the months have passed, Into 16 again
16 I am, and 16 it has been
For this day is sweet and this day is sour
Of the 15 being gone, my 16th has its hour
Celebrate, parade, and dance 16
Dance and parade and celebrate with me
For the days and the weeks and the months has made
My 15 into 16, the sweetest of age.

Under the broken-down bridge
Where we played as kids
Where we laughed and bled
Where we all were fed
As you have read
This bridge so torn
Broken down but built
Of wood and stone, it stands
Where we all held hands
For this bridge so old
So cold in winters time
We sit to propose
Of what we'll always find
We go back to this place
This broken book of worse
This empty page to curse
We enter under the bridge
Where we all played as a kid
For under the bridge, we went And under the bridge we hid
For we knew what it would give
Under the broken-down bridge

Forever Alone

Forever alone, this note I wrote
A note so warm, of words so cold
It chills my tongue, my language to change
Forever alone, I shall remain

End of the road

Even though the road I travel may drink every bit of concrete
We sit our minds more deeply into the sunken broke down seat
Join me down this long hard constant journey
Where life is failed, and truth is covered
For this walk will grant your earnings
And we will finally see each other

Secrets of the meadow

Favorite green rosed dress Lillie's
and orchids surrounding your breast
bright in the light sunny blonde hair with lips
for flowers to bloom when kissed,
but to resist this kiss would empty the mists,
for moist is born and warmth is felt
and in that instant my body melts,
and chocolate coated covered candy continues to spread of sugar so sweet,
so smooth so rich so delicate of taste,
for love is meant to grow not erase,
that place I place my head upon,
your breast so blessed to have you as my one

Alone

I remember when you held me close,
so close to your rose,
so sweet to your nose,

so low to the blow. When you struck me there, I tore my reason to love this season; or the next,

for l am hexed to be erased into space and face the disgrace of an unfinished race.

I am alone and so cold to come home.

I am you, the glue that's stuck to hate and the plate which feeds evil a meal so tight to conceal my heart shut.

Look at me and you see darkness, for my skin to many and to you is so blue and my eyes so black to the fact that life is gone.

And that is the reason I am alone.

Marionettes

The things that they do and the words that they say
and the strings that they pull to continue the play
from a very hot day to the coolness of winter
They walk out the opposite of the same way they enter.
From the roof they hang and performs the play,
so that we all see what was put on display.
On stage they tap, and you see their feet,
The illusion of comedy has lifted the beat.
From their seats they rise like tides they roar
with an applaud so grand it captures them more
For, this stage of talent, full of puppets and string,
of Cotten and wood, this shows we bring.

With fists we fight

Of anger and motion, we conquer you with fists and fury we fight for few
On days of darkness and times of war
We fight and fight for what means more
This journey, this road, this heart we gain from the battlefield of hurt and the suffering of pain
But we march we chant we continue this road
With our fist we fight and carry the load With passion and love and a vision for life
We fight we fight through day and night

Water into water

Deep burial of wet life
out with the old and the new we see
Drowning each sin to begin the fight
to plunder this hate and soon be free.

The sound of a mouse

Rattling of the tail and the hands do move,
feet moving slowly and cheese is its love.
One touch of the switch and the click makes it tick then the tock of its feet
will communicate from beneath.

Your Face

In this place I will erase disgrace and think of your sweet face
For beauty stops and evil fades to bring back the times of better days
Your heart and smile and soul and eyes create the life which never dies
For skies of love we shall improve and remembering moments that do not move
These days are long with years to pass
I embrace the taste without a glass
At first come first my blade of grass, my evening star, my morning rain, my
speck of dust in the window pane

My forever angel

Only Angels come from heaven, but you are the place where I'd love to
visit every moment in my life; your smile of such clear mountain water,
your eyes so adventurous and true, and your lips of plums and berries to
fill my hunger, you're delightful to inspire my broken heart. I'd love to hold
that beauty you possess and capture the true meaning of it All; if there was
one place I'd love to be, it would definitely be with thee.

Bother me evil day

Death of day, night, and dawn
Bother me further my evil spawn
Dread of terror and lifeless grey moon
Bother me further thy poorly month of June
Departed from day for night is the path
Bother me more and feel my worth
Bother me day, bother me day
Bother what I feel, bother what I say
Bother what I am and bother what I've become
Bother what you take and forsake not my freedom

H2O"Hell2Open"

A place where it is calm and cool
A place where it is felt to fill
A drop left to drip inside
A place left to surround them dry
Where heat is present, and warmth is love
Where light is me to give thereof
This lad he craves and stares for care
This land, your land, we do not share
For you state this false ground as your home
State it well and walk alone
Crowd your heart and soul with hate
But I my friend, I will debate
For this land of yours, this hot cast away
Melted into a dreary heart
Take this land and cherish it and alone, for I can't take part

Burning belly of bullshit

Are you done lying, are you done causing this melting of a soul to boil?
With fear and doubt you are dying, bursting into action like a coil
I am hardened by your false words, you inmate mind, your intelligent lies

I am hurt and too kind to be left to die
And that is why I fly into your belly to let you feel the flame I've felt in my heart,
The regrettable feeling unheard of but will take part

Cut the cord
Clamp this cable, this long of a life cord
Separate if you're able to give me my reward
For nine it was mine and now I must let go,
This long of a life love for my cord has come to a close
So cut my cord, divide my support for support I have from thee,
You are the hands I have to hold so cut and set me free

Black and white
White is pure and black is dark
White endures with a spark
Black excludes what white includes
Black forgets what white insists
That sight of white blinds the unblind
They see black, even though we shine

I Remember the Pain
I remember never being home
I remember you there with me
Holding your existence into a bottle of messages
Holding on to your heart to cry alone
And in that place the bottle drops
To crack a code of love or hate
To open the pages of a mystery
And in that maze begins our eternity

The Banana

The shape of the moon, so blonde in its light
And so wonderful tonight
For I have never tasted or felt something so right
The deep feeling of choking and loosening my tight center with love and
pleasure
I do embrace this moon shaped feeling forever
For this hard mushy tasty, delicious and center-filled fruit
Has given me more love and I urge for more to appear from this root

Bored and confused

I am sore demo thinking and alone in my drinking
I am puddle of liquor and a tub of poisoned liver
I am filled with empty friends and feelings,
But my emotions penetrate through this ceiling
And yet I drink or more,
For more bitter drinks I will pour

Birth of destruction

Sink like a lake, think like a lake,
for mouth so dry I can drink like a lake
Bottom of the sea, top of the sky,
One day until night we will run the mile high
Felt from the flood and touched up with blood
From the bottom of the bowl, we will all drip of mud

Passion and pleasure

The angel that took risks to a definition of daring defying dangerous acts
of darkness she is a serpent and she is a damsel in a dress but he is a drunk
and a deadly force of drums to beat like thunder that strikes death of roses
and wine they sip the poison which is given from below and swallowing so
the emptiness of this cup poured strong will cause their love to fade into

flames holding on to each other's hearts, what is left of them, they consume the warmth of it and embrace the fire with passion and pleasure

The vibe of light

I miss the light in the night of a bright vision you took
And look, that simple dream awakens, taken from the same book
You stole the whole vibe inside of my heart to create a hole torn apart
So dreary and dark from the hope of being alive
But alone we are and now I must die
Awaken into the new world to see clouds and seasons changed to rearrange
the light And yes, I am born again of what I write

What do women want

The need of love, but the want of truth
which is more important to you
Thy vows are terrible to the ear but deadly to the heart
for if you start a tale so long then that heart will fall apart
but is it what a woman wants or what a woman needs
of a burden so deep from a lie of the truth
worth dying for of the answer she devours her youth

More than the World

In that moment I saw the ocean, for her eyes washed away the weary reasons to become so blue. With the tint of red and mellow look of the sun, her hair has covered every inch of perfume for it smells so strong, and yet I stood so still to see the pleasure in her lips for they are moist and soft; if the sullenness of her eyes could pierce through each heart, on paper I'd write about this beauty, but she is more than the word we all adore, she is more, so much more.

Crawling in the dark

Pages and pages of white little things
who give the partial credit of those who may Dream
for the faces of double has entered our minds
to forget the harshly truth of what was hard to find

Debt

The value of being poor is extremely the case of an open eye the strong
heart you share will blossom into the biggest meadow of tears an endless
search for a feast or a lake to drink to fill the void of a crying mouth so dry,
but the great idea of this poverty has strength, more of an urge to continue
your cry

Pillows

The one whom I touch
the touch that I feel
the feel that's so soft
the softness concealed
the one who takes dreams
and the screams of disaster
and the one with the drool
before school and thereafter
the one who lays
and the one who is fluffy
but is flat because of thoughts
made from dreamers of an act.
And yet this feeling come
and yet this feeling go
and although she be there
this soft feeling will finally grow.

Owls

On a limb the branch is still
the night is young and the breeze to feel
for we shall look, and we shall hoot,
and if they pass, we will look
With necks to turn and eyes to see,
as wide as they appear, they remain on thee
For we are wing spreaders, and we are good listeners
and we are the hooters of the night with the whisperers
For she is the mate of my call when it's late
and the limb that remains oh so still, she will take
For that mate that I chose and the hoot that I hoot
will be all that I need to make you my new root
And this limb was you, all along only you, not a hoot
not a turn, not a look but the root
you are the existence of this limb that I like
The reason that I love, the owl of my night.

Confusion

Like stairs falling upward without wood to whistle them
And stars so bright they consume the sky inside to twinkle so dem
Of oven heat to sweat we force a nature so relentless
For summer days to scorch the heart which beats the warmth so heartless

Glasses

What's the point in sight when in night the darkness of day preys on the
light of night
Do not blink or think of what to see when the blur of the earth is more
than a wink
More than your vision for permission to see will exist in a mirror of clearer things

Swamp

The liquid you drink and what we swim in to sink and this water is the
amazon of a marsh filled with fish if you wish to just fish but the fun will
be gone so the swamp where we catch a big bass or a croc or a gator with
big teeth where we snag on with the reach of a gun to create this ole fun to
release a sharp shot for a creature with the scales and the claws and the eyes
of a swamp not so dry so when the lives left to live would just swim in the
swamp of the swamp be a swamp then the water would be the world

Shape

Why does she think, why can't she blink
Why must she see, everything but reality
The world is round, and her form is fine
But in her mind, her body is behind
The mirror is her friend, and the scale is her enemy
And pills are the escape, of a walk with agility
But when I see thee, I see the sea
The ocean and the waves, and the flip of a page
Of slim and thin, and beauty within
When I look at thee, I do see beauty

Kinzee

Playful and plenty and packed with a pose
To smile so wild with a twinkle at her nose
And in that twinkle her eyes does shine
Like the stars in the sky where the moon is aligned
With a cry so loud of a siren for warning
Staying up all night and wide awake in the morning
With a bottle or binkie, she sleeps and slumbers
But that smile so wild will stay for the summer

Calendar Days

Numbers we see and plans to be
The day of days to be at ease
Calendar months, the 12 of a year the fear of an end
And will you be here to only pretend
But weeks and minutes and seconds are skipped
Because of a worry where your life was missed

Rainbow

To be gay is gay and why do they say
That I am happy with this day
So proud to stand alongside the hand
Of the light which holds them with water and land
By boat or plane or by train or love
They sing as one to cross the sun
To cross the line of love with clouds
And travel more far with a smile so loud
With a joy accepted to be accepted of their lover
What a gorgeous sight to create some color
We are we fight we stand to be known
To be free to be me to be one on our own

MLK

If my father was here, I'd be a doctor
Instead, I am a tale of many slaves in a coffin
So shallow this hollow grave low and alone
I lay today, today I lay forever on my own
A lash, I feel this scar and this pain concealed inside
Please remember me for what I've done, I've killed the great divide
To bring together the forever peace of one to another we be
A world of love and color we be, so please remember me

On a Day So Loved

Hanging from below and above will I know if the storm will ever leave
A snow so cold an endless December I remember that Christmas Eve
When a cold was wet her care was there but my heart I did deceive
And then we sat to cause a rain fiercer than the Devil's deed
Wind and water and hail and thunder I wonder if she thinks of me
But far away I stay I pray this secret be kept from thee
A truth so shame don't judge my rain my wrath my aim to please
I write to you these flowers I grew to you I send to freeze
A day so grey we cry as one because of a truth made cold
So deep beneath an endless sea of creatures left to unfold
But love, oh love, sweet God above said no!
And light has come
To dry the sky and the days delight of a night to show the sun

My Tears

I am drowning in your tears, I am very far away
Away from the girl who means the most and so I write and pray
To see the face the smile the joy of a twinkle in the eyes of life
Once long ago I met a girl who then became my wife
This road is long so long and rough, but your image gives me hope
I think of thee my forever love, please remember every word I wrote
For the day I pray is hard to handle and the night is full of fear
So, dry your eye, and reply my love a message because I'm near
Not far from you my love is true, my heart is yours to keep
To store forever my forever love, in a place so warm and deep
One day so blue I'll be with you, and forever will I stay
Until then I write, so read my tears of a love so far away

Sally Mae

Sally Mae, oh darling day, what dreams I dream of thee
Of tender lust and evil thrusts of trust from neck to knee

I thirst of moist with kissing you from root to the leaf of life
We venture the dirt of our bodies skin to know that this affair is right
And darken days on thunder nights where lightning strikes the sheets
We slowly make love from the dove above to the creature beneath the sea
I lay with thee my Sally Mae, because our lust is true
An evil deed of planted seeds to taste what once we grew

Wood Work

In the end is a new meaning to the middle of my story
The pages have been flipped and turned and tossed with no worry
But in view the light is new and dry with wood to chop
To make as pages and more to read without the need to stop

The Path

When in the mountain I saw the crack
and down below he broke his back
For curve and slant and slope he went
and continued on until his back was bent
when back was bent he headed on
until time was old of sunrise until dawn
and evening come to melt the stone
until he has aged of skin and bone

Jealous Jewelry

Shining light and frowns of fury,
kept inside to sparkle your jewelry
With shimmer inside a glass of glimmer,
withheld all of the wonders of an unborn sinner

Killer Bee

Killer me, the evil seed of hate
The dirty devil, an endless dream of love left to rape

We take and take and do not break the hate of hell within
But in response this killer bee has given me more sin

She is my nature
In the sky the grass shall grow and so does her hair
As runny and rapid it insists to flow until there be no air
Snow does fall on the floor and more I cry as it melts
As runny rain, it continues to pour of dreams untold and ones not felt
Thinking of things is easy to drink
A glass filled with thoughts overflow me to sink
And in the sky, I can't deny the spring which brings more green

Wreckage
Deep inside the hole of a rotten thing left to drain
A simple spill that can't ignore the cleanliness of rain
To slowly spread the disease of filth I slowly fade away
Into a sea of lonely souls where love will never play
Such cleanly things such open hearts of opera and great song
To explore the world of an empty bottle to capture what belongs

Flapping Feathers
The birds, they sing and chirp and nest
and all the while their feathers flap
Their beaks may buzz, and wings may wonder
while flapping them slowly to fill the summer
With wings in air and sky they fly
and all the while I wonder why
Why do feathers flap so loud
So fearless they are and so proud
They flock as one and spread as two
and sore for more with the love of blue
For love of sky, they fly and fly
And with flapping feathers they fly so high

I'll Never Be

I'll never be what I used to be
I'll never be me
The legs and arms shackled in chains will never be set free
I'll never be the light of love or center of a care
I'll never be what faith has felt because it was never there
I'll never heal from years ago, nor present or futures griefs
I'll never heal from hurt so permanent because of false beliefs
I'll never be perfect, Prince Charming nor a king, nor things from crop to
cream
I'll never be the happy joy, but a little boy of love I'll never be

I wrote to you

I wrote to you, for you, with you
I wrote to you, constant
I wrote and I wrote endless words
I wrote to you, about our love
I wrote and I bled ink to write
I wrote and I wrote endless dreams
I wrote to you my destiny
I wrote to you with hope
I wrote and I wrote
And I write some more
But you are gone and yet I write
I write to you my farewell, my goodbye kiss
I end this to let you know that I'll continue to write

I write to your heart

For you I write, tonight I write
With a smile so bright, with pain you hide
A hurt so deep, it shatters your glass
Piercing the heart to would your past

Your eyes are cold with a heart so weak
For torture has captured what torment may leak
But dear sweet Diana do not hide
For love is near and it will never die

West Side Story

Today the sun has come to greet us
With clouds of grey and winds of gust
The day is new like a baby's birth
Filled with joy and what it's worth
With melted snow and coolness of air
And iced-cube roads for wheels to share
And branches so naked without a leaf
With sorrow for tomorrow and tears of grief

Take me for who I am

Take me for who I am
For I am me
Free from you and will always be
From this misery I have gone
Free from all, thy evil one
Take me for what you see
For I am me
The voice of ink to paper I be from this enemy
I take my air to breathe
For I am me

Cannibal

I am who I am, I am me
The sinful seed, demonized me
Bound to break and swallow souls
This sinful ground with many holes
Take my eyes with sullen glances

And do not run away from certain chances
There is no return once you enter
I will enjoy all of you, my delicious dinner

Illusion of living

I wonder what it will be like in those years
We laugh and play but what will we fear
We age and group together the loves lost
And in this undesirable nightmare a life is the cost
What are green blades of grass which will never grow
Because we paint a different color along the snow
We laugh and play but what will we gain
A winter, a spring, a summer of rain
Where flowers bloom and rivers flow
A meadow of lilies which will always grow
And in this love, we love again
And in this dream, we awaken to pain

What If

What if I had changed, would my life be the same
Into the ocean of ships, to uncover truth from thy lips
As sham spread among my heart
What if we did not part
Would my life be as hard
To bring forth guilt with hurt
As pitiful to me of what it's worth
What if I didn't die
Would wings be meant to fly
Into the dark blue sky
What if it had touched my eye
To see a dream only meant to live
Of pain and sorrow and what hate really is
What if change was but a kiss
But a softness among the gentle touch

Or soothing pressure of more and much
What if this was an angel's lust
A touch, a taste, a tender feeling
Of passion and kisses and heart-felt meanings
Of laughter, so gay, of joy exceeding
What if this change is for a reason

Stolen Love

On the last, before the past, I write to you
Of stolen love and more thereof, I write to you
On this night, before I write, I might find you
Of stolen love and more thereof, my lost soul flew
On the last, before the past, you took my heart, my lonely beat
Of stolen love, and more thereof, my eyes will close, of stolen love

Eyes wide open

I will wake again, I will not sleep alone
For the angel took pain, and sent my angel home
For I am awake, and I am not to slumber
I have been fed today to no longer feel any hunger
For I am awake, with eyes wide open

Dear Megan

What a smile you have and what pain you possess
For you are the one he gave, with love and tenderness
One night it took to see this love
A love shown true from God above
A babe in you, with play in his heart
But that is so new with love from the start
You will be mine, my sweet darling girl
My forever, my day, my night and my world

An Affair

Did I do that to her while she was gone
The mistress thought badly to just move on
She stayed, we played among the door
All of the sheets fell to the floor
We lusted and lingered deep into that lair
To take off our clothes with more than a tear
We are sinners and lovers, an imperfect lover
But we did have the affair, an affair under the covers

The romantic wet scene

I am in my towel sheet, just getting out of the shower
And then you came at my feet, to caress me for an hour
You took the towel away and deeply stared
And in return I felt it soft, a slithering hand across my chest
For my dear heart to melt so slow when both our bodies slowly pressed

Love Gone

This summer rain has given me snow to melt
To abandon such a heart is to regret what I felt
A heart I've found from fallen skies of sorrow
To abandon this sadness is to kill a smile tomorrow
This past has left the earth to bring about the cold
From the beginning of what is new to an end of what is old
When leaves to fall and this wind may blow
A summer has gone for more winters snow
Do not think o seasons and do not imagine this
For words are born with reason and hearts are made to kiss

That Beautiful Place

There is brown all around my eyes and my ceiling is where I am discovered
Many dreams I've dreamt I cannot see; it is a mystery of an unknown lover

A place of mountains where smiles arise, of fields and flowers and waves of
the waters
A place of joy and roses of red, of lilies and laughter with which is said
This paradise so pure placed in sight, this world I have never seen only in a dream
A place of love so dear so near to me, of a joy and laughter, and love which
will always be

My life in her heart
My tears float like waters in the ocean
And so, does this reason to show her emotion
In the same flower she blooms for more
But only if I take her to this shore
A land of love of peace and life
Of angels and honey with care to share
To show her tears for I'll always be there
What is this sound we give to us
A sound of pleasure to treasure with trust
A voice, a noise of one we be
For my life's in her heart for eternity

Satellite sounds
Tune in and turn up to life
The brightest star has shown tonight
From low levels of lost energy
To elevation of dreams within me
Echo this realistic sound, this everlasting song
To reveal something real of what will move on
Reveal your world, your voice, your sound
So, one day we toss, turn, and roll around

Aaliyah(2019)
I met you at age one, with one thing in mind
To create a bond of one and eventually call you mine

I cherished those moments full of laughter and joy
I wish this life to last, the filling of a void
One day goes by and then comes a year
With a smile then created and then follows a tear
I came from miles, many milestones to you
To venture into your heart and to hold on like glue
Miles into three years and another has come
To take you away from me, she's taken more and some
Why take, why break, why make me suffer
Love is what I gave to her and never to another
I am dead, numb, shallow, and some
I'm sorry my daughter for what has come
One day you will know from the lies
One day you will soar so high
Away from the ground where lies are kept
And this love for you is all that's left

Headache and heart attacks

Crumble me into pieces, torcher me into weakness
Devour me with death until there is no more pieces
Turn me to twist, twist me to break me
Killing me slowly, something you've done lately
Cater to my death, danger me to my grave
Dig me deep down, where I can't be saved
I breathe in but never out
Scrambled into worlds without a doubt
More bolts more lightening frightens me
I jump backwards to reveal what you see
I am buried into this life and covered deep
Headache and heart attacks, I will sleep

Your Toes

From head to toe I will let you know
Your hair of gold, how gentle of flow

With cheeks of plums and rose of red
I kiss that hill until tears do shed
Your eyes of the seasons we know so well
To lips of love with a fragrant smell
I touch those clouds with feet of feathers
As slippery as ever, it gets even wetter
With a chest of mountains, I climb abroad
I travel my touch to camp and lodge
To caress and care and charm your arm
To sooth it slowly to keep it warm
Traveling further to your waist and thighs
So close to your toes, I'll make them rise
In the middle of it all my fingers will crawl
To touch the warmth to moisten it all
To the taste of tender legs and finally to your feet
To make your toes curl, my journey is complete

Nature

The root of life which produces a tree
To produce some fruit just like me
A feel of wind, to blow it's breeze
Then fruit do fall down below from the trees
From dirt they rise to stand as foreign
Producing apples, pears, and an orange
The plants and air and water we see
We view it all because vision is free
The vision of life we love in forever
And to love this land we walk through nature

Only the lonely

With sadness and sorrow in their eyes
Only the lonely will know why
With pain and hurts in their heart
Only the lonely can create such art

With loss of loves and drops of a tear
Only the lonely suffers your hell
And that is why I've stay in a shell
To hide away from this hurt
Only the lonely lives under the dirt

Daddy

And now you show a smile, for so long I was tormented
And now you show a smile, you stare to be forgiven
And now you show a smile, I am no longer your child
I am chapters, pages, and novels
Read me with both eyes and follow
And yet you continue to smile
For so long I hated the truth
But dear daddy I forgive you

The Fight Inside

The beat of fear, I rescue many hearts
I hurt no soul, I fight to make whole
A battle of numbers, and the slaying of demons
I cut through hate, until it is eaten
Thrusting with pain, I gain my strength
To harbor love for power
Through chapters of life, I have beaten this fear inside
I have reason to stand, for I am in love again

The End of Sin

You cannot win for your love is sin
You will go down for you will last but one round
No, you will fall down, and you are done
The love of hate, your hate is gone
I am free, I am a spirit
Can you feel this, can you hear it

You cannot win, your love is a sin
I have won, I am his son
I am light and I am love
Your sin are hate, my life is not thereof
I am the fight, the road to light
The flame to the fire, your hate has expired

Win
You will lay down and cry
I'd fight until the day I die
The weight is too much you say
I'd carry the load for the day
"I can't" is in your vocabulary
To me, nothing is scary
Why do you give up
Why let this life defeat you
Labor is never enough
Call on him if you need to
I'd die before I let it win
Never erase the hurt within
But win, defeat, and you will see
That life is what this letter should be

Sealed Inside
This love I show, this love I hide
I will not show the love sealed inside
This smile I keep, with a smile I hide
I will not show, a locked smile inside
This heart which beats, this heart which is heard
It will not ever beat, for its closed with words
Sealed of things and carved inside
Inside I cry, and inside I die

Drift Away

Before I write my life, I paint
Blood fallen until I faint
Sweet life so strong to continuously watch
I will not stand nor share such thoughts
You meant the world to me and took me to the core
Inside of a place that I have never dwelled before
Feel this heart as it beats slow
Kiss me with dry lips and let it all go
I am dead to all who crawl
Stand and you will see me fall
You meant the world to me, and the world was in her eyes
Inside I am dead of love for she has killed my skies

Freedom

Lies of December has frozen my tears
In May I rise to see the sun
I grow more love to spread them here
To find the truth of only my one
So many flowers roamed my garden
And so many die of rootless living
The weeds have cones and pedals to harden
And then a rose appears in giving

September Love

Sarcastic courses of curses which claims me
Haunting me by day and resting in pieces by night
I smile at your game of trying to be me
I crave your attention when the wrong is right
My conscience is constantly coming to claim more
So, I trade fire for love to gain the trust
Something real and pure only angels know what for
For the light and life that lives in all of us

So, sacrificing to lay down a heart of gold
For one who hands small hand to hold
But courses of curses cannot keep coming
Nor can it torment you by continuous haunting
For love is near, it's here to grab
So, take what is yours, a love you never had

The Spark

No time for thinking nor dreaming
Only writing to show why I live
You see words and I see life
Something deep, deep down inside
Below the graves and six feet intervals
You find a substance called love
Called faith, in caves so dark
Until light appears and there begins your spark

Believed in it

Look at what you've overcome
More of many and few of some
You never did give up
Believe in it and It'll believe in us
Fight for them and they will fight for you
It is true, they will do
Do the impossible in many eyes
Give them a glimpse of a surprise
You never did give up
You always believed in it
And so, it has always believed in us

A Road Already Taken

Spilled channels surfed to suffer
Higher bill to pay for a cluster

No sight nor kids to feel
This life is not real
Notes of lies given to hurt
Spilled to spoil and waste in the dirt
Channels passed and truth is faded
Dreams of loves whom I once hated
Leave me, leave me, and never return
Flames rise so the past can burn
Never return, never come to me
Leave me alone and let me be

Our Life as One

Time will turn a coin into riches
And then on the other side will be poverty
Which side to choose, love or death
Heads or tails, we must confess
To complete the task, to pass the test
We must rely on what is blessed
Family, give it all to him
In ways of not knowing, he is our line
Our kiss on the rose which grows a stem
Time will turn it, one day, one night
Which side to choose, either wrong or right
No matter what, we must fight
Not for survival of one, but for all mankind

High In Love

I'm so high so out into a world on a mantle
Something most of us cannot control or handle
Sour systematically into the arms of a murderer
Until you find that faith to know of the burglary
Both have taken a life, and broken into my heart
Not knowing when to write or where to start
I blow my way into your house

I drown every reason to let you out
I swallow the truth and spit out a lie
And vow to love you and to never let it die

Message of Youth

Thumb tap to tap on my toe tips
I handstand on my head to make flips
When I flip to the next script I write
When this pen hits the paper I have sight
Without my glasses I see this world
I saw the laughter and tears of a little girl
What I see is your words, the sound
The system of a bird, this ground
No feathers to fly nor future to feel
No weather to air the sky, nor banana to peel
I am me, I am the day, and you are the week
Stay strong for me and do not be weak
We are the month, and this message is the year
I am the thunder, and this rumble is a tear
I will not fear you, nor will I drop down
I am the pound of the page that is lost and not found

Tree Among Men

They tried to cut me to the core to the end
To the end of my roots, they tried to pretend
From the ground to the sky to the blade
They tried to cut me deep but never could fade
A faded heart which died that night
Fell from the sky like the light in her eyes
She is hurt, she has died, but alive she breathes
Her hair is so long, to hang herself with fear
I am scared to chop this life, for roots are here
Fruits are here, and life is amazing
For among the grave dug, we know what we're saving

Tree among men, we save this life
We will not fall, not today nor tonight

The Everlasting Kiss

There has never been an ocean as wide
The depth of this sea is unknown
Moist has measured its many tide
And that is why thy waters have grown
We embrace such taste and engage it so
To let it slip is to let it go
To love this lust is to hate the shore
So, stay away at sea for more

I Die without You

I search for you, beneath the leaf
Above the roots I do not see
But I do look for thee
I search for you between the lines
Above the bottom I do not see
But I continue to look for thee
I cry for thee, drowning deep without you here
Below the grave, I die inside and disappear
You torture me with your absence
And destroy me with sadness burned
I lost in you and more of ashes
Without you here there is no gladness
I die, I am dead, I am dead my love
Do you care, do you dare or do you shove
For I die without you

Minutes to Midnight

I am tired and hungry
I have to go to work until I am crumbled

It's cold and dark and hell is sunny
But I have to leave for my night has fumbled
Minutes have passed as I write until midnight
I ache for water, but words come first
I write in pen to permanently fight
This demon inside to make me burst

Without You

Without you here my heart may stop
And in an instant my eyes would drop
Without you near my love would go
And in the winter my heart is snow
Without you here I'd die inside
And in that grave my soul had died

Sleeping Beauty

There you are sound asleep underneath my wings
Silently sleeping, slumbering of those dreams
I continue to admit my loving you is easy
While you continue to be silently sleeping
Dressed in black you are my night
My one true sight and darling delight
I hear you breathing, silently sleeping
Slumbering soundly and more astounding
You are dreaming, of love and more
There has never been a dream
Of that I'd ignore, for you are my night, my one true sleeping beauty
And if this dream were real, I'd ask you if you knew me

Rising Sun

My hurt cannot take this love
I haunt your heart but you leave
I've planted this seed brand new

And in return you produce it rotten
I've given more than I've ever given
And in return you create more feeling
Demolish my world for giving you the sun
Destroy my moon for giving you one
Love is not what I wanted torn
And in return hate is born

Once upon a rhyme

Once upon a rhyme and once upon a day
A day filled with sunlight, a day in may
Of flowers and fields and evergreen trees
Of something concealed, but only in my dreams
Once upon a day, once upon a rhyme
A day born in May, once upon a time

My Beautiful Love

When I'm around you I can't help but stare
With those soaring dark
Eyes it compares to the night air
Your smile, so bright, I can't help but imagine kissing you
With lips so wet, so perfect,
It would be difficult for it to come true
Hair of fall, hair I fell for
Those strands which became my grass
With blades so brown, I have found my forever at last

Deep into You

I've traveled this sea for some time
Winds shift, waters roar
And yet I do not cast a dive
to find out what is there in store
I venture around your island

My ship has landed its anchor
My plane must soar
Without a pilot
To risk but more than danger
I am not violent
Nor am I a stranger

My Star By the Sea

How could you stare
To look away from me
I wish to see you dream
To wander by the sea
How am I your sky
And you my moon
With summer days ahead
I wish we were in June
To dream of what you are
To hold what I see
To love what is spoken
How beautiful you are to me
My beautiful star by the sea

One Place

Where would I be, up or down
Where would I be, the sky or the ground
Where would I be, left or right
Where would I be, day or night
Where would I be, dead or in jail
Where would I be, alive or in hell
Where would I be, black or white
Where would I be, wrong or right
Where would I be, if it weren't with you
The one place I'd he will always be true
With you, with you and only you

Love Forever

I know what I see; what I do to be seen.
This parallel problem felt in one.
And now I come to life, the heart of my words.
And in these letters, I have found you.
Feeling of angels and trees and birds.
A love of what will always continue

I Have You

There are not rules in life but limits to life.
And so, with this lavish I will give.
I will gain a smile and lust of everything.
Everything amazing will feel true.
Because I have life, I have you.

Love of Lovers

When we hold each other at night it's like blankets and pillows.
Like the cold so frozen of a baby with a still toe.
That feeling of sadness we don't need but love indeed.
Life with light for we will succeed.
We as one, we as lovers.
In the sun and under the covers.
For we will make love, all day and all night.

I Am Here

Don't cry, do not shed a tear.
Have no fear, have no faith, for I am here.
As far as your heart may feel.
It is I who holds it to heal.
To reveal what love was lost in May.
For June to bloom to see a new day.

The Living Tree

Where is the fruit found, the limits of juices and sweets
The odor of what is given in nourishment.
And you cherish such a tree for I am thee.
I am the life the living expects of age
The smile from such smell.
The page which is read to prevail.
And we combine as one, we grow together.
For living things will last forever.

Love Again

The water has a chill and so does your heart.
With winter passing you continue to place hate into the season.
And why? What reason, what cause do you possess to hurt.
It is evil which blows the leaves across the dirt.
The song which gives a chance to frown, to tear down
To unravel rain and pain, with nothing to gain.
So, it's this stain I remain a writer of you.
A poet of tears, a dreamer of tears.
The same nightmare which brings the chill to my eyes .
To make you love again I write for your skies.

Fear of the Fruit

The tree is split, and the ground is shaken.
The earth is still until you are awaken.
Your fruit is rotten, and seeds are bare.
Until you produce for the use to care.
With insects around you, inside you and near.
It is you the fruit, I fear.
I do not taste what I know could be pure.
I ignore the fruit until there's a cure.

Caressing with Care

I met you on the avenue of hate where you cried into shame.
I filled such tears with care and led you with love to claim.
Without shadows from trees or wind from the air.
I take you to protection, to paradise, to direction of care.

Stay and Never Stray Away

I can't give this heart another beat.
Without you I am incomplete.
So, stay, do not stray.
Do not leave my side nor my beat.
For my heart will fall, it will die.
I don't want the wind to blow away this feeling.
His forever lust for emotions revealing.
For my ships have never sailed this many waters.
Nor have touched the shore as pure as yours.
As soft as the lips that I wish to kiss.
As darling and ear as you are my star.
My day, my night, my forever and more.
I've never met beauty such as yours before.
Without you I die, I'm dead when you're gone.
So, stay, do not stray, for I am your love.

My Love Bird

You turned my world upside down.
You lifted my heart with high beats.
You have found the reason to make a sound.
And in this jungle, I am your beast.
I am the author who passes such words.
I am the nest to possess all birds.
Oh, have given me this kiss, this gift.
The love we share, this heart you lift.
My light, my love, I miss our youth.

When love was new and very true.
Our passion remains, our plant has grown.
And on this night our star has flown.
So, feel this kiss and never let go.
For feelings so mutual our love will show.
For it will grow and show and for you.
My darling our waterfalls will flow so blue.
Because you are my love, my life.
You turn my day to night.
You turn my world upside down.
And for you I have made this sound.

HEAVEN SENT

Heaven has sent God.
God has sent you.
You are amazing to me.
This love is incredible.
My prayers have come true.
And out from the clouds came you.
For you are light,
You are my love.
My jewel so bright,
And none are above.
I love you.

COMPLETE

If you were not my baby, you'd be my onion.
If you were not my tears, you'd be my love.
I cry when you are away from me.
I love the sight of you when you are near.
If you were my food, you'd be my peach.
So juicy when I taste it and so fresh, so sweet.
I bite into this love, and I cry.
Because I've found the moon in my sky.

My Luna, my soul.
You've made me whole.

You are so beautiful

I woke up to a face so sweet.
You are so beautiful.
I kissed your cheek and your eyes opened.
You smiled, and in that moment, paradise.
Your earthy eyes I have discovered.
I see mountains and waters and trees.
And in that beautiful sky is a breeze.
I adore what god has created.
I love this sight of true amazement.
Your body I hold, so close, so warm.
So wet you feel inside, so I hide my hand in you.
For in these heavens cloud we will make love.
We will explore each other.
Whether on top or under the sheets.
You will taste amazing and sweet.
With your hair in curls and lips of cherries.
I hold your neck to make your face buried.
Let's make uncontrollable irresistible love.
Let's kiss, let's love arch other mutually, forever.
This woman, oh my. This sweet thang of mine.
One kiss and I'm in love all over again.
No sin, no song, just action I place upon her body.
I make love to her lips, Ike heaven to an angle.
Like wings to the air, I glide my hands there.
I treasure you; I love you; I make love to you.

The pain of love

The sky be filled with anger today.
The wind, the chill has come this way.
It yells, it roars, it blows with envy.

To torture the terrorize to torment me.
With shelter I hide, I lie out of danger.
Away from harm, I hide from his anger.
He is crying and I do not know why.
So wet, so sad; this opposite of dry.
With clouds so grey and sky covered black.
This feeling felt deep had given love to lack.

Thoughts of you

I see you staring in my eyes.
With those jewels of beauty.
You're shy, you are nervous to fly.
So, I guide your body to come with me.
What must I do to make you want me.
The way I want you is indescribable.
Irresistibly mine, I must set it free.
this animal in me, but a beauty to be.
I remember this day, the sexual encounter.
The food we ate, the hand that felt you.
Your eyes wandered upon me.
But I couldn't let go.
Because this love for your beauty was very true.

You Are

You are my sun, my bright scent of day.
You are my moon, the glow where we lay.
This cool bed of roses has warmed my world.
For more love to be seen for a beautiful girl.
I caress your island with my sullen brown eyes .
I admire your waters along my lonely skies.

Man in a cell

Mostly I sit, motionlessly I pray
For day turn to night and night to day
I mostly sit and then I pray
Morning comes for food and then I sleep
I wake for more and for more to dream
To wake one more to eat again
And in between it all I use this pen

Shaken and Awaken

To realize the push which shoves me
I embrace that fact which loves me
For I was lost in a herd of goats
A lamb drawn to hate to hunger for oats
But that feeling I felt has filled my soul
A push I embraced which made me whole
Like an earthquake or tidal wave, you came
From places to awaken the untamed
For I am shaken by the shove
And forsaken with love
My soul is now healed
From the feeling felt so real

Taken in Angels

She was always the one, my sun and my moon
She was always my rose, which sprung in the month of June
She was always my heart, a vibration which beats for love
She was always my world, my sea, my land, my dove
She was always my heaven, my beloved angel from high
She will always be my life, my forever love, my blue sky

Torn into Areas

Broken down to my last ounce of hope
To measure that simple tear
Has drawn this hate here
To weather the storms with the anger I hold
With a heart left scattered
Has turned my heart into cold
I am torn into areas
And broken in places
So many packs on my shoulders
Has given evil faces
For my heart left alone
Without a beat or a tone
Broken down to my last
Without an ounce left to pass
No faith, no future, no feeling to see
The dream I once had of a man with me
That man, that place, that escape of a tear
A tear of such joy has gone to disappear

Orange and white

I put it on, the criminal I be
To take it off I'd be set free
I smell the taste of white and orange
And in my cell my mind is torn
But orange and white I wear tonight
Until morning and evening drinks are poured

A flower so pure

The growth of you I remember
I saw your smile in December
I recall and I remember
The color so green in the winter

Your eyes captured me like morning light
Your love brought me to a new sight
For your smile so bright and your shine I remember
That winter beauty which was in December
You grew and grew and gave me life
A flower so pure I cherish tonight

My two daughters plus one

My two daughters plus one, they smile so big
So much joy with fun, my daughters sure did
Of beauty and laughter, with love and more
My two plus one, the girls I adore
For Gabriella, I miss
And Aaliyah, you too
And for my plus one Ma'Kinzee,
This love is for you too
If only a kiss, could I give to feel
My lips to their cheeks, my love to their lives
I'd give if I could give, I'd give it, no lies

My only one

My only son, my Ryder die
Father and son, I can't deny
Like twins we be, just you and me
My only one, my two-year-old son
My ball of fun, my yarn untangled
My fall created, to give me an angel
A smile like mine, a mind of more
A boy so real, I do adore
My only, my only, my darling boy
My Ryder, my son, my only joy

Dreaming of Her

Dreaming in the day and daydreaming away
Of you, of her, of a lady I knew
Of a woman I knew and grew to love
More love than shoves we gave to shove
More riches of kisses we kissed like this
To miss your kiss, I'd kill the stone
Of a girl I knew who is now gone

A Boat Set to Sail

Are we ready for the ride of the tide
For this wave will not stop nor will it hide
I hold thy hands of a grip to not slip
And our eye on each other, to uncover with our lips
For this sea be great and this tide be high
With my hand in yours we will not die
But we will fly, and we will soar
As we have never done before
Above the tide we're set to ride
Because of the love we store

The Island across

You chose this land, but my ambitious on
You choose to travel for a thousand suns
To a moon so bright, so big you see
To travel abroad, why not for me?
I'm here so come to me my dear
For I am your island, and I am your love

My Lady in Orchids

Surrounding this beauty with colors, with love
I cherish my lady in orchids

To scent and smell we dance the day
Into the orchids of children to play
My lady in orchids my lady you be
Of the prettiest of colors, your orchid is for me

One window cell

We share that shine, that spot we sit in
With you in my arms, we often visit
That spot we see that cell we sit
That shine we share, we be a one window pair

A shout in the night

Stop and do not do this to us
We be together and together forever
Why must you turn our vegetable to rot
Why must you forget what you already forgot
For I am right here, right here in front of thee
Why do you go for what's greener when I'm on this knee
Begging for love, showing you mine
But none you show to me
I shout about, come to me my dear love
For together forever we be

Heaven is a place in her eyes

A place where meadows grow
A place of flowers and roses
Where life has turned to snow
Where the touch nibbles at our noses
I gazed among that winter look
Those green medallion things
Those wonderous things of pupils took
And places I've never been
A field to run and play and dance

To dream underneath the skies
To learn of true and happy romance
For heaven is in her eyes

The sweetest woman in the world

In her eyes are the greenest grasses
The places where animals lay
And in her mouth are words of truth
I dare not get away
In her smile a twinkle sits
A place where stars exists
And in her hands are sands of love
I dare not ever resist
In her care, her breasts of warmth
The place where my head will lay
And in her care, I will be there
To never ever stray
In her heart I won't depart
the place of love for this girl
the beauty of life, my darling girl, the sweetest girl in the world

Door of Faces

I sit in this room and I sit
I see what I see of faces I see
Words they are and words they be
A door of faces to fit
And that is why these faces I see
That is why I sit

I create to make you appear

This image of purple I create I create
To mold into blue of an image to rate
Do you like this look, this gentle stare

I create what I see for you to be there
This form I have made, to form and to mold
To create what is paved, do you see? Look, behold
Such beauty of an art, such song left to sing
To create what is true, this beautiful image of you

The irresistible angel

Someone so hard-headed but someone true
Someone so loud yet she is new
Someone of feeling revealed
A love that's healed
Someone sweet and not sour
To taste would be to devour
For as pure as she may be
God made her just for me

Sacrifices

I dedicate my life to my wife, to my wife, for my kids
And for my kids I dedicate this, no matter what secrets she hid
I dedicate my love to only thee, for you and me, for my family
For we be trapped, and we be free
Forever I'll fake this dedication for them, for eternity

When you know it's her

When in that moment, that little glimpse
Of nervousness and I haven't any sense
I cannot think, she has my mind
A rose among the others with many vines
She is smiling and all you can see is joy
And you, a man, curious like a boy
For she is my winter, and I am her fall
To bloom in the spring, her hands are small
That smile she has, that touch of tears

Has given more joy to turn into years
But this night, this moment I see
When you know it's her, your wife she'll be

For Your Eyes Only

For your eyes only
And for your ears
It has been centuries of lies
And a river full of tears
Winds have blown below
And the sun has shown
For this truth to grow
For what is unknown
Your eyes were closed
Unaware for years
But the season arose
For the truth to appear

My Only Valentine

I am so amazed at this heart, this love that I posses
It was there from the start, this seed planted deep
From the ground to the sky, and that is why I keep
And never do I deny, such love and life be filled
To fill my inner youth, of a flower hath yet revealed
This love is eternal, dreams of passion to never be lost
For we are one, together, and true indeed, yet never false
For I was saved by love, by a wonder, a miraculous miracle
And in that embrace, we share a hug, like understanding the meaning of parables
We both were down below, bred underneath the dark,
To sprout of something to grow, to approach with just a spark
I reached out my limbs, my stems were stretched to the touch
And that is love from him, a love so loved so much
I write this night, to read this day
To share a love of light, which rose in may

To rise into hearts, to embrace this joy
The gift of a start, from the love of a boy
The ones who are close to you, do not take away
Because their love is always true, from the night of sleep to the wake of day
From the wake of day to the light of night
And love is my day, the reason why I write
Do you see the tree that grew, with fruit to fill the soul
For this is what we always knew that together we would be whole
That simple seed, that love of hope, that creation in our heart
Has given thee and also me, a love that will never part
For this love is pure, this gentle breeze of morning
Felt quite right to endure, the everlasting touch so warming
But if you feel unloved, if you feel so cold and alone
Come to his love, a love thereof, and call his invitation into your home
For he is love, the truest of all, the light, the way, the one we call
When feeling low and down of fear, he lands his love within your ear
To hear a love you've never heard, the beauty of songs given to a bird
For he so loved the world so dear, he gave his son to us
His love will never disappear, like the wind when it stirs the dust
For in this trust and in this heart, bears the fruit from a simple bark
From a tree planted deep into my life, for this valentine I write will be tonight
My valentine, my love, my dear, my only, my day and night to live as one
and not be so lonely
Dear valentine, this heart of mine, this joy brought on this day
To call it mine, my valentine, this love I love will lay

Row of Roses

Gather in my garden and consume this space
For row of roses are compared to her face
And with roots so strong her beauty is real
To capture the lost so that love can reveal
That image of many, like comparing the rose
to place in my hand, to sniff with my nose
such fragrance I taste and tenderness placed
of the row we compare to the beauty of her face

My Pleasurable Rose

I know what your naked flower wants,
the essence of pleasure from your eyes
which sights the overlapping touch of my tongue
and every minute of unbearable grasps
of my hands placed upon your petals
for those slender limbs are the greenest of green
I embrace the dew which I've placed upon them
And I love the rose which sets upon them
For that flower has been in lustful encounters
But none such as the one I give tonight
For in this moment, you will sprout for my pleasure
For my touch, for my tongue and for the kiss I give to you

Naked Paradise

Opening your legs I have explored love and I have felt paradise within your thighs
While looking into your eyes, I venture deeply
Pleasurably, and without question with more heat in my lust than ever
Which has been spilled into the deepest chapters of your novel
I read over and over the things which have been causing you to moan
And lust for more, I love to touch your sacred jewel
For it shines brighter than any sun
It glows more than any moon
And it is embraced more than any dream worth coming true
Thank you, my love, for this paradise world of yours

Why I Write

I was the part of paradise that gave light
That gave love to write
To write about life and my pain
And that pain is what put you in spite
Despite what happened I must write
Because I am that part of paradise

Blended Pain

I felt that rain fall down deep into my soul
With spoons and forks I could not fold
To relentlessly leave this storm I hunger
I thirst so I drink the juice of hurt
And I remain a part of that dream
I remain alone without love, without them

Into the pages of my pain

When you read what I wrote do not cry
For the storm is near to fill the sky
Do not shed one tear my dear
For the rain is coming oh so near
You see the lightening and you hear the thunder
And that is why I thirst, that is why I hunger
For my pages are pain, the loneliness of rain

Mind of a Free Man

Unchained and set to sail, and free from this
Free from bricks, free from hell, free from it
Free from the early wake ups and shared showers
Free from the filth, the smells of controlled hours
Unchained of shackles and set free from cells
Free from the walls and the dirtiness and smells
Free from the mind of an inmate to
To fight and begin the mind of a free man

OLD MAN BLUE

Old man blue
The things that he knew.
From grapefruits to stew
He knew what to do

He took a cook book
And yes, he did cook
He's tried to look
and dipped and shook
But old and blue
He knew what to do
And on his break at two
He'd grab him a brew.
The things that he'd cook
When he flipped through his book
Dressed fresh from head to shoe
Was the man they called Blue

SMILE

A smile lass a while
Then it fades like a wave
Then stops like a watch
Like a race with a rapid pace
To face odds of few
If only they were two
Two odds added in
To place a smile within

I Love You

In the last part of my life,
I hope to be with you.
Underneath the stars,
Laying under a big tree.
Me and you together,
Holding hands with love between them.
For nothing will separate our souls.
And no one will enter our bed.

Smile with me as we venture
Further into the ending of
Our lives for we shall enter
The beginning of paradise.
I am yours to keep so hold me tight
And remember this heart.
When we close our eyes for the last time,
Search for me.
For I will be waiting on that side so green,
That side of life here love never ends.
For the love we have shared,
Under the stars, under the big tree.
With our hands together.
With love between them,
And with all that we hold dear for each other.
This love will always be.
So, begin this with me and I with thee.
And the love that was born will always be.
I Love You.

ALLIGATOR DREAM

Once upon a time I woke up to see,
An alligator looking to snap at me.
With the teeth of knives, it snapped some more.
I tried to run but fell to the floor.
Rapidly running it came even closer.
I jumped back from him and rolled right over
I grabbed my pillow to cover my head.
He stared at me and crawled under my bed.
I closed my eyes to open them again.
I woke to see that it was pretend.
A nightmare I had, so I write in my pad.
About the scary dream, it was just my dad.

HOW WILL THEY KNOW THIS MAN THAT I AM

For the years of knowing them,
And the day which were some.
How will they remember me,
And know whom I've become.
For the years have passed
And the days have gone.
How will they know that I was their only one.
For they only knew screaming
And they have only seen fighting.
How will they know the meaning
Of the truth of my writing.
Dear Ryder and Ma'Kinzee,
I hope you one day see.
The man whom I've became,
So please forgive me.

STEPS TO THE RHYTHM

First step on the bottom.
Two steps now in the third.
Threw steps to help me to six
My way to seven, then heaven.
On the fifth I write about that line
To the sixth again to create this rhyme.

SUBMIT TO THE WORLD

Submit to this feeling,
For the world is polluted.
With the crime of hurdler and stealing.
Allow me to teach and you be my student.
Submit to the music.
The sound of the ground.

Surround down to the loud.
Pound for pound we will leave.
Allow this world to fade with a breeze.

PURE ART

What do we do without wisdom.
We work hard without wisdom.
No mind needed use labor.
No thoughts wanted, no genius.
We succeed on what's written on paper.
To create our natural genius.

DESTRUCTION

City of lies town of the dead.
Dreams of no emotion,
State of no regrets.
Lonely place in her face,
A crooked smile to erase.
Drowning in silence to kill,
Pain is what we will feel.

MOTHER NATURES FEELINGS

Your tears fell on the ground.
I picked up that rose.
It sprung up from the rough,
To smell in air without a sound.
Taste that of rain drop,
So salty it drops for love.
Grow me more to cry,
And then their bed no more pain.

FUEL ME WITH FEAR

Fuel me with fear for I am fire.
You dump me in coals to lift me higher.
You spread my love with darkness,
This is why I burn what's in your chest.
A hole to fill with water of none,
This love of fire has just begun.

TORMENT

As gorgeous as ever seen,
I cannot feel your skin.
I cannot touch your eyes tonight,
Nor your hair so thin.
Your lips are curved in perfect shape,
And in this pain bears your taste.

MISSING PIECE

In your eyes you're a window.
Silent bright and dark to answer.
Door bells and knocks but you do not open.
You are the only identical cancer.
You hide and run but tears continue.
Your disguise is powerless against my heart.
You want to live within me,
Be my puzzle and always be.

Overcome the Dark

Lost soul surrounded by black day.
Run away from light in the month of May.
Hide and do not make a sound,
Nor crawl but sit upon a hard ground.
You find words to speak,

Yet I do not understand lies.
Your lost soul is very weak,
Like the small body of many flies.
Stay here with me and keep the faith together.
You and I, we remain safe.
Come out of darkness and promise to scream.
With the light of love your souls are now free.

Walking in that world

Be gentle, do not slip into the abyss of life
In a world where wrong is right
Where good is bad and bad is worse
And in the pure lies are a darkened curse
Do not fall short of the longest lie
For the longest lie will cause you to die
To live in strength, you cannot do
But to die in weakness, that is me too
So, stand with me, walk this world
For I am you and you are me
And together we are, together we be

The last sightseeing you

I was so close to work, on Airline I drove
I saw a face pop up as I looked over
I saw your smile, your small hand held high
I was so happy, I did start to cry
At that moment I felt like a dad
And to my son I write about on my note pad
I'm glad for his creation, I hope one day you see
That I was there all along, right there with thee

In That Flower

In that flower I have found pollen
A smile so pure where tears have fallen
Tears of joy for pedals to grow
In that flower you are exposed
A color of colors and smell so sweet
The sweetest of smells, I fell at my feet
For in that flower, I have found thee

Surrender to Her

To surrender with you, we let go of all that we have felt
For our bodies to be warm and to one day melt
Curled in your lust and caught into your eyes
I venture towards your legs while gazing into your skies
The moist of your lips, the scent of your hair
I embrace this sweet gift with each moan that we share
For I am your captive, I serve your body forever
I will not try to escape for we belong together

This Broken Stone

A broken storm has caused a storm
To bury the winter to keep you warm
To drown in pieces of dreams of hurt
A broken stone buried in the dirt
To company my soul of bitter cold
To store for later when the beat is old
A broken stone compared to my heart
Break my bones, in my grave I rot

Death

It was so long ago, when the fresh water hit
A storm fell upon my heart, and in that spark my night was lit

I followed that road of hate, and darkness came after and murdered me
Barely seeing, I fell, and into the blood I became the sea

Free in Love
Fly high and do not fall
Save your future with a smile
Dream of it all, every season
Summer is amongst us then the fall
But do not fall for hates reason
For you are beautiful, all of you
Never forget what I write
Never forget what you read
Love with all of your might
And in love we will always be

L and P
Paradise in life, lingering in peace
Pain in living, paralyze my legs
Lessons in pressure, patience in learning
Levels in progress, partners in love

Memories of you
A figure of frames, a portrait of peace
A castle so calm, a rest for my release
My love and my life, my all and my feet
My dream in a painting, with a portrait complete
My past and my pain, my time of many tears
My meaning meant to remember, to enjoy all of these years

Fly my love, my lovely dove
A bird landed on the shoulders of my heart
Chirped in my ears so I'd hear the harp

Played a beautiful tune just for me
And now I know it's sweet melody
I sit in hell until I gain my heaven
To write my talent with song of blessing
Chirp away my friend and reveal thy love
And in the sun our moon will rise
And in thy sky, we fly above

A heavy sleep

Made deep to drown with monsters around
I do not exist in this world of black
I do not feel what could be found
Made in depth with less to lack
Like drops of blood to be cleansed
Or dirty grounds to be swept
The existence of life forever sinned
And in return a void is kept

Mind of Faith

Think of me as a gift for I write for us
I have years behind what I lift
And in that past, I torcher trust
From day to day, we preach it so
And word to word this anger will grow
I dwell upon hurt and also pain
For life is built on terrible things
And upon this drift we die again
And this is what our life may bring
I write and I write, and I suffer thoughts
Yet, an independent soul knows no loss
So, I fight, and I fight, and I conquer fear
Until the day of grey slowly disappears

Close Love

Sound asleep, my love has been
Silently slumbering without a whisper
Surrounded by stars and darkness within
The promise to love thy brother and sister

On the other side of the mountain

Every step we took could not be repeated
This road, the heavy loads we crafted so blindly
I gather all of this energy to delete it
And into this world I enter with wings
Over this mountain must be sweet
For this side is dry without taste
We wander yonder to find that tongue
To taste the race and energy to run
Landing on the top, conflict to approach
We regain ourselves; we gather this rope
Hope, we have until rain and snow
We, hand in hand, step by step, we grow
Over this mountain, almost to be the bottom
I breathe that breath to go
In the end we made it, we are one again
Hand in hand, one step at a time
We have crossed that finish line

One or the other

Outside is warm, with a ground so hard and rough
Breeze will blow and bound with bodies
This 2020 life is tough, and faith is being lost
We are losing our loved ones, outside in the cold
The ground is untouched, for gravity is present
Are you ready to taste the air and venture into heaven?

What did I do

What have I done to you to make you hate me
Karma is crazy, didn't know she would be back
To torment my world, I have to come clean
What did I do? I tortured my future
Killed my past, to suicidally write my future
I do not imagine; I have a reality of fears and failures
What am I to do? You have taken from me the most
Now I feel empty, no smile nor pain
Numb is what I have become; what have I done?

Eyes open and eyes shut

When I saw your rose bloom I knew it was June
A month of heat and also rain for more to consume
Gather all the flowers and gather all the fields
Of gardens with lilies and orchids to reveal
Colors of life, choices of love, to conceal this with light
Until the weather turns to snow, and then my roses will surely die

September Became May in a Day

One visit with lights and sounds around
A dark room of news unknown and not yet found
With news to know and waiting to see
A boy or girl for you and me
Living on the edge with excitement and joy
Hoping things go my way and that we'll have a boy
I remember your face, I saw you smile
And then it came true, Alejandro is our child
Kicking and moving, he is our baby boy
Until more news hit, to hurt and destroy
Our son was fun, innocent and true
But from big feet to small, my pain then grew

Our baby will be gone to heaven with God
Our September became May in a day with the swiftness of a nod
In May on a day so close to my heart
Until we meet again my son, today we will depart

God sees us all
Of all the stars in the sky, we do not see the light
We hide in silence of knowledge unknown
Our cloths are not nearly sown
What little faith, no hope to ask
We want it all without effort
We do not pay the price to grasp
Our loves, our sinful pleasure
With eyes wide open we run and hide
We do not see the truth
Of lies we hide, we never forgive
And in turn we destroy our youth
He sees us all, so do not fall, but crawl back to the stars
Of light, we come from dirt from birth, to travel our love to mars

Going in Blind
When will you see that I've always wanted
From a dream to reality, my life is haunted
I bump into obstacles and corners
I wish I could feel this pain
With sight of an incomplete foreigner
I am in obligation to clear the stain
This is my December, a time to go blind
This is what I remember, the thought of you in my mind

Into the darkness

You fall down on your knees to choke
Your voice is sad and says death
Your words are belittled by my eyes
And above all things you take away hope

I Love You Forever

I see those days coming in slowly
Like the moon so cool, so bright
At night she sleeps with burning light
This evening love sits with me holy
How swift is the wind with smiles of joy
Vast glances of life to remember this so
For more dreams we share, for rivers to flow
My hand will reach for you, for my kisses to enjoy
And in that moment my ocean opens
My waves embrace the sand
My words for tears to land
Deeply, so low into this love
So much love, I love you forever

Nowhere but in your heaven

I had nowhere to embrace my words
My careful words for loves eyes
I drown my heart with you
If this life is heaven, I'll see angels
I'll see you there, surrounding me and covering my pain
Breaking this chain slow, and loving me again
To live in your heaven, I embrace you slow
Holding you forever, and never letting go

I Care

As much as we are known to kiss, I inherit
To lust for your lips and venture towards
a mountain of ice, So cold so frozen
our love for life is our forever reward
we strangle the need to miss one another
hour after hour has passed with patience
to pace and pace until your face is there
as much as we are known to love, I truly care

Field of Flowers

In a field of many flowers and lilies
In a dream of many sacred mazes
In a world of waves to tides we ride
For I have yet found my peace
No sleep, remorse for what is done
But I do embrace the breath of the sun
We walked that mile, we dreamt that dream
We kissed each kiss, with crops of cream
And yet, I do not sleep, I do not scream
I do not love, for my life is rough
This road is long, and curves are sharp
This field of many will create what is dark
Now my lilies are grown and my flowers are in bloom
For my love has shown with a glow of the moon
My dreams are clear, and my world is ridden
With waves so high, your love is given

Peruvian Princess

From afar you are my shooting star
I could not let you go
I could not let you disappear
And here you are, my beautiful shooting star

Those eyes, those lights within the sea
Those eyes, those silencing waves
Built within was a grin
A giggle, my Peruvian friend
From afar I saw thee
The ocean's waves blew towards me
I felt your waters wash against me
That feeling so wet, I do not regret thee
My Peruvian palace, my dear night
So beautiful were those eyes, so bright
I took that leap, that smile
So deep, I dove into your Nile
My Peruvian princess, my sweet love
From afar you came, like an angel from above

Love the Most

Love will always come for those
whose anger persists the most
Love will always come to those
who welcomes their enemies
before their loved ones
hate is the hell which you host
so, love deep, love the most

A Love I Loved

I saw your skin within the clouds
Your wind be gentle until the wild
I smell the scent of your milky breast
I want to caress them I shall confess
To taste your flower, I want to do
And in that hour your eyes are blue
To turn them green for grass to grow
I'd turn them around for love to show
Your hands, so soft, so small, so sweet

I'd hold, so tight, so blessed to be
Your lips are cherries I'd love to eat
Like bites, so ripe, so wet and sweet
Lay with me by the moon or mars
To venture so far for passionate scars
I taste your skin, your garden of roses
Of red, of violet, of life unspoken
I want to taste your heaven so much
Of life with purity to bear such touch
The day your eyes turned green to blue
I knew this love would one day come true

Love for Hate
Some days I write to remember
Pain struck the month of December
You killed me inside and thew me out
You drowned my heart without a doubt
But in that pain, I surely gained
A love for hate which still remains
And n that hate I gained a trust
To hold for hate, to latch onto lust

Calling the Night
Where are you right now, when my eyes are blinded
I ask for your shadow, but you are simple-minded
In time of need I sit in the sun
Soaking in heat until I am well done
Wanting only, you, the coolness of life
The darkest of days, they call you the night

To Michelle
The sea is in your smile to spread
And smile my love, you are no longer dead
But alive like eyes of grassy plains

Or blue of sky with no more pain
A butterfly so beautiful with wings of gold
The body once warm has gone so cold
But now eternity is in your eyes
Smile my love, ands always rise
Like the sun and moon, and other light
And as beautiful as day and as lovely as night
Close your eyes and sleep in peace
In heaven your soul has been released
My dear Michelle I'll see you soon
Among the love and light consumed

My RAY of SONlight

You are high above and distant from my earth
My heat unknown ever since your birth
This line I write for your eyes to one day see
I thought of you when there was no gravity
The heat below to blow my age away
Until then my twin continue to warm the day
To heat the beat with something sweet with all my love to lay
Until your light reveals the truth my sonlight of a Ray

Sweet Water

Do you taste me, I am cool and slow
Take a breath to breathe, My love will flow
Dry heart of fear, Pain to follow every step
Come to me, I'll be here, through heat of hurt and every depth
Stay with me in coolness and care, pour this cup and I will be there

Look at That Mat

Look at that mat, you sit on me like I'm black
Sliding your shoes on me, you knew they were dirty
Look at that mat

I welcome you but you scatter me, why not just let me be
No acknowledgement and no care
Run me over like I am not there
With you two dirty pair
Look at that mat, you sit on me like I'm black
We are opposite but still, your shoes are too rough to feel
You claim to be so pure, so bright, so white
Then why do you stain me with darkness of night
Look at that mat
I do not dare call you names
I'm still to the abuse you put on me
But look at that mat you've just turned green
Brown and black, "what about you?"
Do you wish to be as black as blue?
A darker color than what you are
You are similar to those of a star
Look at that mat and then look at me
If I am flat, then you will be
If I am dirt, then you are brown
We both are objects on solid ground
So, look at that mat, for you too are black

A family we bee
There are bees among the comb
A place so sweet to call a home
A food of choice to prepare
Come with me in the air
We travel to plants and also pollen
Find things we have in common
For survival we gather this color
For sister and for our bumble brother
For a meal later to eat
There are sweets in the tree
Come with me to feast inside
Into our home we call a hive

Crawl to walk

I grew up with hip hop
Surrounded by hard times
Fluent now to hard rock
Beats of sounds is on my mind
So lost and abandoned in my past
No feelings through the year nor a care
I finally see what I should have
The sweet and coolness of your air
No more hard times, no more abandonment
Only sunshine, and love from my family

Why Me

I'm all alone until you come
What made my thorns appear in your garden
Why not choose a stem which bears no harm
Why me of all things you pursue upon
I'm lost and lonely until you come
What light is shown to reveal my name
Why not pick roses of lilies for view
Why me of all colors when my heart is torn in two
Why me I ask, why love the dark
Why make me cry of truths to spark
With dreams of freedom from hate and hurt
Why me you place in heavens dirt
Why me?

I am sorry

You bring me to my knees with thoughts of doubt
I am wrong of my past but why force me to shout
I hurt you with pain by stabbing your heart
But why not understand that I want a new star

I am done of bad to begin the good
To share with you my love
To give to you all the things I should
My goddess from above

Robin Hood

Steal from the rich to feed the poor
To give to them so they'd have more
I stole her heart to give her mine
To give it to her, my love will incline
To plot the plan to save a life
We took in wrongdoing for the right
An idea to care for the life of another
I gave her words like there is no other
And now the poor are no longer in hunger
On top of the pavement and no longer under
This girl I made dear would be my thief
To love the poor souls and to save from grief

The Life

Why must I sit here and dream of hate
Why must I wake to a nightmare unreal
Untold stories are your beauty to tell
Why did you save me from that hell
Why can you smile when there are clouds
And inside your heart there is a frown
Upside down, your symbol of hope
Why did you hold on and not let go
The steps we've traveled and boundaries breached
To the moon and back where gravity is the least
Every tunnel in time and every mirror seen
I realize this world was not just a dream
You gave me the stars and ocean to feel

To wash the wave, I could never touch
To understand the reason this love will heal
And this is why I love you so much

E.T.
Eventful evening even everlasting
Everything enters entirely everything
The time tends to travel towards them
Til the turn trembles there
Elastic energy entering
Entirely everything emptied
Til time tears the truthful thought
Take this thought then travel there

If I was white, I'd be red
Blood here rushes towards my head
Heart pumping, with a beat skipping
No longer silent, no longer empty
This smile you give me has never been shown
Nor has it been given, so far from unknown
My face chocolate covered disguised to be
If it were white, it would be R-E-D

First Kiss
Wet warm willing touch
If only I knew this lust as much
How pure and soft it was to me
Roses bloomed in spring that day
And the grass so green and a sky so blue
I still remember the day I kissed you

Underneath it all

Under the ocean, my love has drowned
Under the waters, beneath the ground
My love has vanished, under the tides
Beneath all traffic, beneath a crushed love
My heart has been broken, under all of this surface
My love will no longer open, unless hearts are worthless

My Dark Secret

To cheat on the love of your life, why hurt what is pure
The struggle of joining hands with her
The reason she chose your smile, why cheat on cupids choice
When the dream you've wanted has come, why destroy her voice
When the love you need is there
To cheat would be unfair
Why a deep dark secret
Why this hurt and pain to bare
To give your heart and soul to her
To show her your love and that you care
The secret you keep will trip your feet
You'll lose your mind and your sleep
And when she's gone what will you do
Why do to her what she could do to you

Soft Reason to Survive

A pillow we preserve to lay our head
As a flower smells of happy smiles
To deliver joy for a mouth which hungers
And a heart so warm to open the clouds
They do not know how we feel inside
To stumble and then open arms wide open
To place the care of love on our dreams
And a pillow to give us what is chosen

Devices in this clock

The crank and continuous clanks
Into the mind of time to move on
Screws within will turn your days
And in the night the long is gone
Gears are slow like a broken heart
Some ticks may sound because of scars
Those tocks like rocks are hard to throw
This world is a device we do not know
A puzzle to put together for time
To understand well in every rhyme
A tick or tock or granddaddy clock
To watch, we waste our time a lot
This world is a clank or a crank to turn
To create a device in your life with concerns

Princess of Pain

As down as the ground her frown has grown
A princess of pain who drowns her crown
With loneliness from the loss of a love left alone
Thy lady is hurt from the emptiness of one
To condensate her tears with a kiss or care
And to not dry eyes with whatever there are
She sits in silence until someone arrives
And rescues her heart where fire lives
A knight unknown to her eyes so green
To rescue his love for love unseen

Forever in Love

For time and time, I sit and drink of pain
I swallow the gulp of an endless rain
The poison has surrounded on me it's brutal force
Upon my longues I choke much worse

The wet ground I stand to step about
And in this reason, I kiss your mouth
Embrace of stares we share this feeling
Of pain and pleasure to plan the revealing
None will be left unsaid
To bring the light to the day
And everything that is read
Will be for the beauty of your lovely face
I remain here to forever feel care
A love so deep we knew it'd be there
Forever in love, in love we be
Forever with you, and for eternity

Us as One

When you left, I cried, when I wept I died
When we kept our pride, no longer could we hide
The love we have, we could not save
Not at that moment, but what is there to vent
Why are we a fight, why are you the day
Why am I the night, why lie awake
We are a rope untied, we are tangled inside
We are a dream of gold, with hands kept to hold
Do not unfold your mind, let us not unwind
Let this love remain
Let us as one always stay the same

Down in the Depths

Deep depression does very deadly deeds
Down in the depths is where they maybe
Darkening days during durable dreams
Depression is the darling which drowns the seed
Depths drug down, deep down under
Under a world of suspicion and full of wonder

Damage in the Flames

The colors are yellow, do you see them spark
A light so mellow, then an orange to start
A touch of red, you burn in hell
We dine to death, can you tell?

Ball of Yarn

We of string, we tightened things
We stretch our strength, to expand our wings
We have no limits, but a ball we be
Of yarn we're close and tangled, not free
We twist and bend and wrap around
So fuzzy, so long, we touch the ground
A world we are, confused and bunched together
So close yet so far, but we remain with each other

My Thoughts of Love

I will position my thoughts upon your mind
And we will both have what it takes to find
To search for a peace so true, so new
To search for a relief, a place so blue
To sky we be, the ocean we are
The star so far, we shoot for par
For birdie for eagle, we shoot for love
I position it all on the beauty thereof

Your Eyes

When I saw your eyes, my heart said "you"
You are the one to ease this pain
The pain from days where my heart was two
Torn from a bolt of lightning with rain
Those blades of green grown in meadow

The simple silence of a night so cool
Where spring is born and leaves to blow
And in your eyes bears a jewel
A pool of blood I'd lay my head
I'd fight to see those eyes again
And stare in them until I'm dead
For they are paradise and love within

Back in Time

Moving slowly in an open field of lust
That's the place where I lost my trust
The many different demons who came to me
Are the very little reasons I'm in so deep
This place of envy and darkness I travel
To find my way back to 10 years unraveled
Can I come back and be that sea
The one who grew, the tree of 3
Laughter, love, living is my past time
I must put it on my heart and also my mind
To be free from hate and hell and hurt
I will leave this place of the filthiest dirt
Moving rapidly to gather my steps to you
That is the place where dreams come true
Your face, your smile, your touch of wild
The feeling felt real since I was a child
From a time of romance, my mind was there
And so now I travel with wings in the air
To gain that trust, to outcast the lust
To bring back the 3 which created an us

Falling Upward

Falling upward to my depths in heaven
I fell asleep in time at around 7
On a calm cloud we dream

On a cloud we sleep
We slumber so deep
On a cloud of cream
Taste my heaven, my home, my happiness
And in this tree bears my nest
The rest of it all is there to see
While falling upward, we are set free

KJ Love

This song stuck in my head is dead
But the lyrics are seen with everything red
It whispers on my heart of memories born
For memories to die, this song will cry
I will fly away from you both
As I swear, I will keep this oath
I will remember this love of lies
A hurt which had me blind
To find my sight of mind
And fly into another ones skies

The Beginning of Love

From what has begun my start has sprung
Like the blooming of flowers or words of song
In class we crawl on stage we stand
For winter made Fall to freeze again
The hibernation of months, the life of snores
The closing of cold to behold open doors
This chapter we start, this page we turn
To create our beginning to cause love to burn

Walking in Wisdom

I will never forget, I will never quit
I've held on tight, I've come too far

For you I will continue, for you I'll love
I made you; I gave you life
I am your author, and you are my light
Without you I am faded
Without you I am lost
So, I traveled to be near your smile
It took me many agonizing miles
With wisdom I walk
With you I am strong
With this pencil I will talk
And write the mistakes of my wrongs

New Surface

This sight of the sea has seen many surfaces
From beginning to end, this life was worth it
My days for weeks made my months into years
Those moments made real has created these tears
The sun to set has gone to a life eternal
To shine above new surfaces of a different journal

Depths of the Day

As the time pass by, so does the wind
For more to bestow in the snow to descend
In this sun and in this moon
We feel time has passed to leave here soon
To venture into the clouds, the place of peace
To lay in the depth of what has made deceased
Of what has made new and true to paradise
To create more peace for pain is paralyzed
The permanent picture painted for life
As the time pass by we enjoy this sight
For depth of day and love to endure
We venture there for life is pure

Nail of Thorns

This long endless doubt of painful rust
Has clouded my pain back into the dust
Stone after stone to slay the sin
To cast out enemies and demons within
You drug your dust unto the wood
To kill our sin to show us what's good

Love is Living

Live with me and love in peace
In peace we live and love we give
Let us embrace life with wings of joy
Live and smile with light to deploy
Spread this world with each beat
With each piece of rhythm of your feet
Shout to the world about your girl
Stand if you can for the love of your man
Live free and be for you, be for us
Be with trust, but love it all
Love so big and love so tall

Your Last Chance at Tears

And I thought this would be it
Me and my tears beginning to fit
I show my emotions as you embrace pain
I want to feel and not be dead
Paralyzed by loves choice to consume me
And that is why I am free
I wanted to cry, to shed a bed of rivers
And oceans I drown but God is to fear
He is near, do you stand or do you bow

With the last chance of tears, do you act now
Your last chance at tears
Let them shed or let them disappear

Sin Cebollas Para Mi Corazon

No onions for my heart
For tears do fall thereafter
Her heart is torn apart
And there no pieces gather
She smiles for miles in silence
In peace her voice is buried
Her heart has been through violence
To see it keeps me worried
Sin cebollas para mi Corazón
So, continue and we will move on
Para Corazón may make her cry
Para Corazón may make her die
But departed love has torn her heart
And tears do fall in the deepest dark
So, smile in covert to continue to move on
Para sin cebollas para mi corazón

The Poet of my Life

The light touched the dark, the ground disappeared
The sun rose without fear, my love has created your heart
My day, so gloomy and empty, the sound of a kiss upon my eye
the echo of the other to open the sky, the love you gave is now in me
my oh my, I cry with music, my led, my ink continues to use it
the path leads me to lines, the place where your beauty has been defined
my love, my love, you're given me grace, my joy, my led will never erase

My Chances

What have I done to you
To throw away such a view
Wishing this disaster was clean
And begging for your dreams
With nightmares of faded trees
They blow, they whisper along the wall
My chance, my choice, has bled the call
You're gone, you're far and out of reach
To each their own is what I teach
But take it all, never leave behind
For someone to come and again to find
The love you've left to leave you in pain
Your chance to love, your chance to gain

My Juliet

I did not know such beauty could blow
For time will spread for a rose to grow
How soft her pillow, I lay mindlessly there
And in this comfort her eyes we stare
For days are more as I gaze at thee
For more to come and more to see
I woke that dawn to arrive on air
We flew through clouds beyond compare
To tear our reasons, we think of few
For love to grow to create a new

Days in the dark

I've spent days in darkness and days in sin
And months in turmoil for years I bend
I break my silence and tear my page
For ink do shed and tears of rage
So many words, so many battles

I've fought against it and now do I tattle
I am blind of light, dirty in doing
Away from grace because of my choosing

Poetic War
Long day fell on nightly lines
To venture into space beyond the times
Back in, back then, behind the sun
My sweat fed the body by the ton
I bled, feeding another day for pain
To gain disaster and create the same
I planted roses in a garden of thorns
So that you see we both exists where we are torn
This day, this night, this led I write
About the times my lines did fight

Flight of love, journey above
Where did I find you, where did you find me
Where did we find us, where will we be
Where will we land, the air is clear
The charter is full, our love has flown
Into coolness of clouds
We found us, among the rest
I found trust, you've found me
Devoted, we love, we land,
This journey began, when you took my hand

Find the Love
Look at us, we play this world like it's ours
Full of fools we be with disgrace of powers
We turn the other cheek to show we hate
No care for one another, no love at this rate
Why do we let him win

Why do we love such sin
We embrace lies with feathers of few
To create our crash to crush what's new
Look at us, we pity the rich
For poor souls are dying and liars' mound to pitch
Are you struck because the cock crowed three
Or will you lift a soul and save us with me

Struggle in the Bubble

Take a bath with me and wash what is filth
For sinners are winners if you admit your guilt
Come in air, in the thickness of all thin
With love upon our hearts to cast out all sin
Come to clean your soul, clear your mind
Control the hole to feel what we find
Together we live, together we be
Clean and without struggle, in this bubble of eternity

The memories are seen

One day I will go blind
find me and tell me the time
One more time, let's play this life
To rewind the day, you shot that three
Come on the court and play with me
And day I will not see
Find me in the crowd of hide and seek
One more time let's play that game
To keep the past alive and our youth the same
Come with me, for this hope I give
To enjoy my sight while I still live

Gone too soon

Every freezing piece of rain will ice the heart
To walk across this endless pain would not take part
You'd die before a step, before a breath to breathe
Abandoned life for death so soon, depart this life and leave
A journey fought with youth so young
And not one chance to dream
The dream of love and life to come
The fading into what's never seen

I Hate

I do not hate you for what you are
Nor do I hate you for what you say
I do not hate you for something in thee
But I do hate you because of me
For the monster unleashed has caused a fight
On thirteen days before Christmas night
I've planted a seed which continues to grow
So cold, it grows with veins of snow
Cold-hearted I be, yes, I do hate me
This shackled old beast must not be set free
I've tormented your heart and killed your soul
Fractured pieces so small, you will not be whole
For I do not hate you for what you say
Nor do I hate you for who you are
Nor do I hate thee on any day
But I do hate thee for my fallen star

My Rarest Rose

You are an undying rose
A beauty who hides her love
With dark seductive eyes your pain is shown
And in this desire your needs are known

I've seen your disguise, your reason to run
But do not hide your beauty from the golden sun
Your lips, so soft, I dare not kiss
For if I do, your heart I'd miss
Your hair so dark, I'm lost and tangled
But within that forest bears a beautiful angel
You are a rare rose, with skin of sand
To journey across your body, I'd venture your land
I'd travel my hands across your sea
But of such beauty, you must be free
This pain from your past will harm you no more
For I am your ship, I'll guide you to shore
I'll grasp your hands and hold you close
And whisper in your ear to call you my rose
I'd lean towards your lips to give you a kiss
A feeling so real I would not miss
A touch so wet I'd kiss your neck
With your mouth wanting more I'd taste it next
Your eyes are closed shut, your embrace wide open
I hold your neck firmly and continue going
You are my flower, so I water you with kisses
To give you this moment and so many wishes
A rare beauty you be, outside and in
To make you feel loved, I'd do it again
I write you this poem, so one day you'd keep
And store it within your heart, a place very deep

Living isn't so bad

After the storm hit my heart
I slumber, I sleep, I silently sit
Until someone tells me to never quit
Dreamers are lovers and lying is a sin
Never give up, for faith is built within
The lights turned down low
Dim and empty without a glow

Oblivion and death began our path
Broken on foot with shattered glass
Believe, behold the new day
The light has come on a winter in May
Heart pounding for more and life is good
And love is given as it should

Mama

If you could see me now
As high as you are, can you see me now
Can you reach my mind to know
To know that I've been missing you so
I miss you mama, always have
Now we are on better terms, but also different paths
I remember your smile and also that pain
But no more pain for you, only love to gain
Goodbye foe now, if you could only see me
You'd smile, because I am also with thee

Hate to Love

I remember my past, those eyes
That stare, that glare, you did not care
We were close, connected, calculated to be together
You did not hesitate to love me more
And that is why those lips I adore
Those eyes, dark sullen slithering eyes
A ray of roses to fill my skies
I did not care to love you furthermore
I did not hesitate like once before
Quiet as the air I'd stare
As you walk by with silhouette hair
I did not waste more time
I had to make you mine

I came to you, looked deep into your universe
I saw the stars, the ocean, the sea of love
Push me closer so my lust would budge
I need you; I want you, I crave you
You are so dangerous for me and I for you
This feeling will sink into my life
This love will fill my skies

In the water

I look into the ripples
I see your smile and also your heart
A place I saw in the start
My planet stops for gravity is there
And yet you care
I stare into your eyes, your heart and soul
You are the piece to make me whole
I love you my love, my lady, my forever
You and I together forever

To surrender to you

To surrender to your heart
I cannot resist this temptation
Those eyes matched with the sky's of heaven
Those lips created from the clouds of God
With a blade of blonde to shine upon

Extra Love

I began this road, this walk, this heavy load
I stretch my heart into the pond
With heavy feelings of toads and torcher
Casting spells with an enchanted want
Only to stretch further beyond the border
If only your hands could pretend to be here

To land alongside my heart without fear
I would venture into your field
With an army of love and steel
Feel my love, my heart, and soul
And one day you and I will be whole

Along the Lines of Love

There is a line drawn to protect a sweet beat so pure
I caress the outside while embracing what's in
I do not allow clutter around this town to tour
And that is why the line so thick surrounds the love I spin
Along this border I must protect to invest my all into
Such beauty of a beat of life she be and with this love I prove

Honest to say

I can honestly say that you are going to go to heaven
As for me, maybe not so sure
I used to be sweet at the 7/11
But now I steal all hearts that are pure
I drown them with coke and fill them with juice
And in your eye, I take the sight
For love is gone, there is no use
To bring about the day or the light
I am but a gloomy heart of darkness dead and dumb
Honestly, I'd say that my love is numb
To hope for a man to walk with a head up
I'd give you a headache and tell you tough luck
But for me to walk into those heavenly doors
I'd have to surrender the hate and the love of whores
For me to enter God's good grace
I'd step on the line to begin the race
Honestly to say, I am tired of the hate
I am tired of tears and the fear of a heartache
Honestly to say I'll take back the coke

I'll surrender the juice and repeat what I wrote
To drown what is pure, to endure what is true
I would not hate honest to say, I'd have to love you

One Nem Ones

If you ever heard of this before then notice how they act and feel
They are something special and will tell you whatever is real
They are known as such to do the most
One nem ones to break the rules
Always wanting to brag and boast
One nem ones, the dumbest of fools
This phrase is for them ones who do not care
The ones you know who are called the Karens
One nem ones to play truth or dare
Always out running errands
Now you know about them ones I speak of
One nem ones that need to be beat up

A Lady I Knew

On the streets of New Orleans there stood a wonderous beauty
An elegant young Saffire whom I called my lil cutie
She winked at me every day when I would walk on by
And in that beauty, of my lovely cutie, I saw that twinkle in her eye
So sweet, so innocent, so wild with her luscious lips
So juicy, so layered, so thick she be with her dancers hips
I couldn't resist that kiss she gave but it was in my dreams
A kiss so real, so wet but still it wasn't what it seemed
For reality hit and the cutie I knew was just a fantasy
An illusion, a mirage, a mythical love, a lady who will never be

Click Clack

Clicking and clacking, tipping and tapping along the keys to play a note
A rhyme a rhythm a beat so sweet to read whatever the author wrote

They criss, they cross, they wander the surface
They venture the keys with just one purpose
I tip and tap and type the words to give to you my love
A blessing, confessing my life on paper this talent from above
Hold this art and never part my click to clack my note
The greatest rhyme to look upon, so sweet of a beat that I just wrote

The Eagle in My Sky

She soared so high and swooped so low
I never knew those wings could give such flow
With eyes so sharp and claws so fierce and loud
I never knew her love for the air could pierce through clouds
I'd love to travel with her and be her sun in the day
I'd love to travel with her and be her moon at night
She soared to my heart on a day in May
And ventured into my world with all her might

The Horse with Remorse

In the hospital bed I sat so sad, so alone I sat, so drowned in tears
With a bruised back I laid, so limp and low, I put my hand there, in pain
and fear
From the farm to this bed I broke my leg, I hit my head and killed the air
I made love with the dirt and felt a force of pain to only compare
I looked up and saw a face, a man with big teeth with arms so strong
I looked once more and saw a tear from that ole man's eye for all the wrong
I was dazed and dizzy, didn't know what hit me but I finally came to
Of a force so fierce, so heavy so strong I realized that it was all you
Not a man, nor my trainer but a horse you be
A horse with much remorse with the power of three

A Spiders Love

Your heart is on a string.
A web of confusion to swirl.

A line of love you bring.
To spin contagiously around my world

LOVE FROM HER

Love is lies of life to live.
To linger in love, we learn to give.
Leave is fear to fall down deep.
To fail in love my hate becomes steep.
Love me dear lady and live.
Linger here with me and I will give.
To not fear love, do not fall.
I will give you everything and my all.
Forever and always; simply in love.
Beautiful someone; my darlin from above.

Broken me Down

Paper in my hand to hurt your heart.
Pencil writes down hate to break us apart.
Beginning this goodbye, I sent so simple.
Line four is rocky but is written by my pencil.
As you hear, it stabs to cause a tear.
To tear it apart, the beat will disappear.

IN HELL

From hell he came and started a flame.
Of rage and war, we fight for more.
Red-eye demon with fire to roar,
We find the hell what he made it for.
Hot pot boiling to melt my soul,
Devils' child play to kill what's whole.
To rip the pieces of a heart so cold,
To bitter the sweets of what was old.

From hell I came to write my fire,
Come with me forever and I'll inspire.

Life is the Light

Life is your light of love to live in luxury with me.
I become too quiet with feathers and soft spots.
Tear down this shadow and open up the sea.
I am the love and life which s set free.
I am the life in your light as you wish to be.

MOVIES IN MY MIND

Picture me in your head.
I am a monster under your bed.
A nightmare you wish to see instead.
This is why my poems are read.
This is why you smile to see,
To vision this all in a dream.
To slowly think to imagine me.
Movies are not always what they seem.
So, picture me now in your head.
Before you lay down to go to bed.

NOWHERE SLOW

Didn't know time flew like planes.
O lightning bolt run when it rains.
Up to speed in bold of pace.
And flight of feet to win the race.
Trees grow slow like nowhere fast.
In electric time I write like flash.
Dashing forward at sewing machine speed.
To give you the pace of words that you read.
To strike such lightning in skies so dark.
So nowhere slow will darken this spark.

MY PAST IS GONE

I am no longer harmed by you.
You, demon of fire who comes in dew.
You, wrath of hate who challenges rage.
I am no longer the ink on this page.
I am no longer the son of silence.
You come to kill with miles of violence.
You come to claim the right of flame.
I am no longer of your name.

MAGICAL ME

In a glass jar of lottery tickets,
I granted well to play my wishes.
I threw the spade to win the game,
In the end my friends remain.
In the light I lift my wand,
I crack a joke to lay upon.
I center pieces to play for keeps,
In a glass where beaches breath.
In a circle fans shall roar,
I do not know what on earth for.
I guess this glass is breaking free,
In the end, I am he.

CAPTIVITY UNTIL ACTIVITY

What will happen when we believe?
Do legs fall off with fatigue?
Do hits feel pain with our bricks?
What will happen when it sticks?
Do shadows talk and scatter illusions?
Do animals speak with diverse confusion?
Do humans remember with memories?
What will happen when we're free?

The first heart to break

I took the sucker on that night,
And swallowed the taste of poison?
My life changes after such night,
And forever ruined many choices.
That morning was cold, and it hurt.
Bruises and cuts are my heart.
I cried out for help within the dirt.
And that is how it all took part.

TILL TIME AND BACK

In a clock of ticks and tocks,
I found my bleach to clean the spot.
Til time has come I learn.
I twist the hand for its turn.
I earn the minutes of each second,
And that is my life's lesson.
In a world of space and air.
I found a way to live there.
Life is over and gone.
I twist to the hour I'm on.
Til time and back I write.
I dream of you every night.

FIRST SIGHT ON THAT NIGHT

To infinity and beyond,
We sat beside that pond.
We held hands on that night,
It truly was love at first sight.
Warm palms, tender touches,
Your heartbeat is like double duchess.
Looking into your eyes was forever,
Kisses and love under sunny weather.

Can no one take away that feeling,
You lift me higher than cupids ceiling.
I hold your waist on this surface,
Being with you is my only true purpose.
I am yours alone and yours to keep.
I love you like an ocean, a place very deep.
I'm glad we made one on that summer's night,
I'm in love because of you and that's why I write.

SELECTED BY BEAUTY

You called my name,
That everlasting sound.
You opened my eye to gain
The everlasting love
I've found has spread deep
Into me and filled my world.
Of lights, life, and things to see.
The image of a beautiful girl.

NO LONGER IN LOVE

Empty bowl of feelings.
With sky's dry as sand.
To equal the value of few.
With nothing left in hand.
The voice of a whisper.
With blank thoughts of you.
And nothing left to give her.
With the lonely value of few.

A SINNER'S MIND

And on that night, I saw hell.
A world of angels I dare to tell.
A dream of water I drink to swallow.

And on that night, I didn't follow.
The trees were waterfalls and oceans ice.
In fields of nourishment of being ripe.
In valleys of winds to feel forever.
The place of angels where I call pleasure.
And on that night, I saw life.
A world of demons I dare to write.
A dream of fire I touch to turn.
Nd on that night I did not burn.
The trees were coals to only inspire.
Considering that love to set a fire.
In flames of heart to die in seconds.
The place of demons where I call heaven.

EVERYTHING IN MY EYE

I see the ocean out there.
So red and clear; I cry.
I see the blood and hair.
So, red until I die.
And in my heart, I see you.
That beautiful view.
I cried a little more.
I wish I had four.
But I only have one.
Because my vision is the sun.
So blind to this life.
So unsure of the sky.
In writing is what I write.
About everything in my eye.

LOST IN LOVE

Til I die.
I will love,
Til that day.

I will live,
And then I love.
And love; and love.
Finding a way here,
And losing my hate.
No longer owning fear,
And I will love.
Til the day
That God given day.
I will say
"This is love"
And so, I love.

RAGE OF ROSES

I spill my love with this.
I will your hate with this.
I caress your neck with this.
I undress my heart with this.
You embrace my love with this.
You disgrace, your hate with it.
You discover the feeling of it.
Beneath your feet they flow,
Above your skull they show.
Within your life they live,
And for this girl I give.

DARK ART

The color of fear
I darken here.
With smells of charcoal,
I fell in this hole.
Black area of sin.
We perish the chance
Of closed eyes in storms

Hell creates romance
Pierce painting of night
Instant death put to rest
And in dreams there's light
Until we gasp our last breath
To show deeds of such color
To live deep in such state
I create the ravens brother

TRADING PLACES

Why do we fight.
With fist of mud and feet of white
Why do we fight
Th hands of powder and throw of dirt
Why do we fight
We hate each other in fear
So why do we fight
Why do we fight
My people use dirt
And you use powder
So, what is the point
To see who has more power
If you strike, I turn white
And I strike to turn you brown
In the end we will blend in the ground
If I get hit by you
And you get hit by me
Then mud would stain you too
And you would then be unfree
And in this hate I feel your pain
Your ancestors gave this world a stain
To you I give my mud to see
It is you who's imprisoned and I am free

ODOR

The smell of it is new to lovers
Peoples who haven't experienced it
The feeling of pain cannot heal
Can it not be tamed with one touch
As you can see, I am cold as ice
I am alone and that is why I smell
I am dead to love, can you tell
I am anything bad and nothing nice
The smell of hurt, I cry
I am alone, so I had to die

ALL AROUND THE WORLD IN SEARCH FOR A GIRL

North, South, East, or West
Which would be the best
To find that star which shoots past
I want to find you at least.
I wish upon such beauty to see
If one day you come to be
A pair of loves to love indeed
In years of a hurt so hard to bear
I could not weep or shed a tear
I tore into and lost my heart
Which landed deep in the dark
Until that night on search for you
Not knowing why only a question of who
But you my love, my savior from hate
On a night so real, our very first date
The light of love the Jew, my pearl
All around the world, in search of a girl

REALITY OF DREAMS

Daddy was gone until candy came
Put it on the fridge is what gave him fame
It's what he did that didn't count
What he didn't do made love drown
The birth of revenge and date arose
Roses of evil all around my nose
You made mama sad, you left
The choice you made is greed on the shelf
All grown from that month
April left me on a slump
I jump to a new life of love
Writing about every push and shove
Read my story of life and do not blink
To think of my words is like our favorite drink
The rebirth of a poet has come
As ripe as all the juices in a plum
Read my life and yours too
Because dreams do come true

MISERY

Walk on me, is that your fight.
Step on me, is that your elite
Throw punches at face
And that will be your biggest mistake
Surround my heart again
Crush every bone within
Bring out the devil in me
And that will be your misery

OPEN UP

Spill this hurt upon m ear
And I will hear

Spread this love til it disappears
And I will hear
Silence darkness til its clear
And I will hear
Surrender to love and have no fear
And I will be here

HARMFUL LETTERS

Dear Nicole
I lied; I am your friend.
This lonely world I live in pretend.
I smile when you speak
And hugs are like a shark's feet
Not real nor visible to my eye
Our moments together will surely die
Days of dancing on darkened flowers
And nights to cheer with you more
The stabbing of my back you have given me
And it took away, love to be my enemy
Your ex BFF

NEWBORN LOVE

Complement the waiter on his work
So fast and your feet hurt
So quick of eyes for movement
Your passion is based on a true event
We tip for service and smiles
For love and kindness, you spread
For drinks and food were fed
Like the care of our unborn child

DEAR SWEET KISS

I am embraced with this
Gentle touch of your lips
So precious of a gift
So real inside my life
A world of untold secrets
To remove truths of lies
And dear sweet kiss, do you keep it

DANGEROUS HEART

You never cared about my boys
Words of purity was no choice
It came true by hurt
It came without warnings
You never cared from the start
No, my love is severely harming

DECLINED OF LIFE

Nobody wants to be with me
My haunted life of misery
My sacred eyes of the tears to fall
Nobody wants to hear my call
My heart is crushed into bits
My breath is taken away
Nobody wants any of this
Nobody but death will play

ONE MORE CHANCE

Before you go, let me apologize
Before you leave listen to my vibe
Before you go, I want you to realize
That if you leave my soul will die

Make this real no more suffering
Nothing bad, nor the other things
Before you go thing to stay
Think of the one who loves you this way

NEVER CAN BE USED

I will never lose
I will never abuse
I will never lie
I will never cry
I will never fear
I will never compare
I will never divide
I will never hide
I will never fight
I will never write
I will never hate
I will love my fate

TO SLUMBER, TO SLEEP

In a slow slumber I sleep
But I do not dream
I do not move or toss or turn
I do not shiver when leaves to burn
I am still and no breath I breathe
I am a stone with the weight of trees
In the slow slumber, I am calm
I do not shake by the coolness of my palm
I am connected to this paper
From this nest to the savior
I am somewhere anywhere, but here
Somewhere far, not near
I have disappeared into light and air

One day you'll see me there
Because in a slow slumber I sleep
If heaven be water than I am deep
I am asleep in a deep sleep
Not in the dream, but I am this sheet

REASON I WRITE

So many times, you wanted me to stay
I've tried to run through life and just play
I scatter my thoughts till I cry
The pain is so strong I could die
Hold my hand to the contra peace of life
And there you'll see the reason why I write

DYING LOVE

If I had a dime, I'd feed you two nickels
Not anything sweet just wrapped pickles
On days of grey I'll call the sun
To feel the void of darkness fun
I pace to the steps of the soldiers march
To walk alone, alone in the dark

TRUST IN GOD

The beginning of an end
I find a true friend
From lost to found
My trumpet has sound
I begin this feeling
Of life untold
To life I find meaning
I finally feel whole
My soul is alive and guarded

I am here to tell my story
To finish what I started
And give God the glory

The Beginning of Love
From what has begun my start has sprung
Like the blooming of flowers or words of songs
In class we crawl, on stage we stand
For winter made fall to freeze again
The hibernation of months and the life of snores
The closing of cold to behold open doors
This chapter we start, this page to turn
To create our beginning to cause love to burn

Walking in Wisdom
I will never forget the darkness, but I will expose the light
The darkness gave me danger and terror and fright
I will let that feeling go and enter into a new
A world of spring in wintertime where our roses grew
I will stand as tall as I can stand and walk towards the truth
I take a step and a few more breaths for wisdom has made me move

A Broken Man
He is but lost and only she can find him in this abyss of cloudy days
He searches for a ship to come and rescue him from the mist of castaways
She is there for him, yet the winds are rough, and the waters are rugged
Only she can help him escape from a broken heart so ugly
The pain he endures from the cold and dark nights pushes him to wander further
He cannot see her, she's so close to him but the broken man has committed murder
He's killed the heart and crushed the soul of a woman he loved so dear
But she is near for this man of fear to forgive and love I swear
I tell you all, hold on to the love which God has placed in your hand
For dear sweet souls behold the untold story of the lost and Broken Man

Her Illusion

I embraced her with arms so open and free
An embrace that gave her me
She never suffered from pain or hurt
I never let her feet hit the dirt
My lover, my sweet life of tender care
She was the song so sweet I could never share
My life, my love, be here for this beauty
A long time ago my lover new me
But now she's gone from my lonely sight
She vanished one morning while it was night
Her lips were silent after such day
My lover has slowly drifted away

My Lil Darlin'

My queen of a cowgirl is always on the ranch
Roping all the cattle and swinging from the branch
Jumping in the creek at least 5 times a week
Riding like a bull in my F150's seat
She's so pretty and genuine, so wild and free
She's the queen of all the girls whom God gave to me
When she cracks that smile, oh boy, you best believe
My Lil Darlin' of a lady sure got love for me

My Son Saint

My dear son saint is as innocent and sweet
He's wild of a child with a rapid heartbeat
With a bush for hair and with big bread cheeks
He's built to last like a future athlete
Born on two three and landed in March
This kid stays crisp like pants fully starched
With a smile like me and a frown like me
My son Saint is gonna be an OG

And I love this kid, lord father knows it's true
My son Saint will always be the boy who made me new

Camping Time
On a Wednesday we'd leave to get ourselves a spot
No signal by the trees and for sure the sun was hot
We walked for a mile, and we'd spin all in the dirt
With the four-wheelers we'd ride, with or without a shirt
In June it would rain and in July it would shine
And in August, it'd fry you until your skin was dry
September felt like December, getting all cool and such
But man, in October, that breeze would freeze your butt
Throughout the day I'd drink a beer and soak up that good ole yellow sun
We'd skip the rocks and cross the bridge
Or kill some snakes with a twig
We'd tent it up and watch a few of the animals emerging to enter
We'd wave to the neighbors and drink some more before we start our dinner
So loud at night we'd enjoy the stars and howl all at the moon
I sure can't wait for summer to come to camp at the start of June

She Loved Him
With all her heart and soul of gold, she gave him her very all
Her world was crushed on the day after the raindrops came to fall
He stared away on that day she could not say goodbye
He cried inside but so did she because she just stood by
What could she do what could she say when her guy was there to see
Her mind was racing her heart was too when she knew she had to leave
She left the mountains to enter the bay on a day so wet and unclear
She loved that man, that forever land but she had to disappear
And now he's gone, he's away from her, and now she must move on
The man she loved did love her too, but his forever girl was gone

The Last Fight of my Life

You took them once, you took them twice
My oxygen levels will pay the price
I heard them call my name today
A sound my heart uproars to play
Beat by beat it works for me
Waiting for answers to set them free
For oxygen to flow and for love to be shown
But I sure wish that my kids weren't all the way gone
My life's mid aged so slay me away
But do not suffer my life today
So young, so innocent, so wild and free
Held captive by you because of envy
I check my pulse, so high, so beyond
And because of the fact that they are gone
I do not understand it, I do not live
Without words, nor rhyme for this fight I give
To the last breath, without a pulse of air
I'll find more oxygen, in heaven or up there
We will be together, for this fight is life
Even if I must, my oxygen will pay the price

The ultimate shutter

This is the ultimate shutter
The wind has blown into another
The blades of grass has cut my finger
This departure of skin has given me anger
A cut so deep it made me suffer
This is the ultimate forever shutter

A time ago

Once upon a time there was a word
Such word was beautiful, just like a bird
The grooves of a lady, the color of her too
Those fine markings reminds me of you
Your eyes are as dark as night
Your lips are as big as day
Your hair so tangled, into hands
Your voice so strong, your love so strong

Your Rose

Roses are red, violets are green
Plants are purple and so it everything
Sugar is sweet and I am too
No love is greater than the one with you
I surround your mind with lust
Scatter your words like dust
So sweet, your blood I taste
An endless love with haste
Your vines so strong and green
Your rose so red and true
Your love to me is everything
And loving you is all I'll ever do

The Creation of Me

It was you, all of you, who has created me with a gift
The gift to write, to rhyme a line without the flow of a beat
Without the air to breathe a breath, without the words in my head
You place a world in my heart for my readers to know that I am fed
With nouns and verbs and similes and metaphors for the soul
You've formed me well with this gifted spell to love your heart so whole
Read my mind, and rhyme with me the words stuck deep inside
And do not fear my lonely tear before I write my lines

So, sing this song and read along the metaphors and similes
I give to you my creators who have given me these wings

Let it all just happen
What will come will be
From the sun going up until it all comes down
It will come to thee
No time nor clock nor chime to watch
It will come to thee
What will come will definitely be

A Thousand Tears
I have written over one thousand dreams
I have put down on paper every pain
I have told many stories among many
I have more memories to tell
Give me your eyes
Give me your ears
Give some to the wives
Give an ever tear

A Brown Pair of Pants
Chocolate in my pocket
And I had forgotten it
I put my pants in the washer
And then in the dryer
At first the sky had paints of blue
But the chocolate in my pocket made something new
A color darker like the skin I'm in
And golly, I got a new pair of pants

My Kiss

On the shore of nowhere I found you
A sunny day so quiet, and summer day so new
With those eyes of red and hair of fire
And skin of silk to create more desire
I could not spare the moment to be alone
To wander around with a home
I could not bear to be away
From your night nor your day
I come to thee to prepare a life
A place of forever, a place so right
So new to me, this love you are
From the nightmares of dying to living within your star
I remain unseen, unknown, and without this
But among it all, I've found my forever kiss

I Love You Too

A secret kept deep, so discreet
The love I loved is gone from me
I cared so hard and drowned in tears
My heart pumped blood for the one who made it beat
I bled my silence and endured my heart to break
For you I loved so widely, and my forever girl has escaped
You grabbed my heart and took this tear and turned it into dreams
But when you left your hand detached far away from me
I think of you, of only you, my dear sweet love of mine
And one day soon, down the road, this love for you I'll find
I hope that day you can escape the place you now call home
For I know in you, you felt it too, the love we called our own

Seductive Woman

With eyes so bright and full of light
So full of truth so full of lies

Once made blue of sky, now grey
For manipulative storms to get her way
She screams, she roars, she shakes, she cries
She seems these sores may break our skies
But with those eyes, those pretty eyes, she shows her seductive side
A side so clear and then the tide begins to rise

I walked for miles

I searched for a place to lay my head
I lift my eyes to look for bread
I thirst thereafter for purity
I begin to walk to find these things
For miles I walk to gather life
From day to night, I gather life
From night to day I search for ink
To write a letter to my dear old feet

Tears into the Ocean

All of the many dreams have turned into a nightmare
I swear, the ocean is among the pain of many who has taken us there
They wander the land to a hole so dark to shed the many cries
Of a love so loved by them so deep the pain has emptied the skies

A Vampire's Tear

We have suffered with each other, and among the suffering we shed
We bleed, we bled the reddest of colors, and among the bleeding we are fed
We drink, we dream, while the cave is all in silence
We think, we scream, while the slaves of thy neck cause violence
I wish, oh I do wish, to drink of death instead
For taking a life within this light is something that can't be bred
The bite I bite the birth of more, I give to bleed of fear
My love for death has given life to this vampire's tear

The spaces between us

Mars has landed on my Earth
Love has given birth to my heart
Stars are granted to eyes of you
And the moon in June will come soon
For my Venus I cry a Saturn's ring
To place there dearly upon your finger
A sight of colors only space can bring
And the universe I have to bring her
But my love, my sweet Jupiter, my Juliet to be
Is so far, so far, so far away from me

Can you do 10

If I do 40, can you give me 10?
To venture into a land, a place I've never been
Can you give me 10 and be my dear friend?
A land so sweet to me, while the image is pretend
My mind is set on 50, but my eyes are placed down low
For when I start feeling dizzy, the 10 I ask I hope you show
So, if you don't mind, please surrender 10
And for you I'll remain, your dear Mr. 40 of a friend

The Milk in My Mouth

An out-of-control bowl you are, and I am your silk
A soft small blend of white with a touch of lovely milk
A drink drunken slow of such with thin, with whole with skim
A drop to stop the dryness of mouth to satisfy within
My mouth so full because of you, my darling taste of white
You fill my bowl and then my mouth and entered into my life
The milk of silk, the white so pure, my drink I drink so slow
I care for you, because of you, you've filled my empty bowl

Nobody Told Her

She settled for the first smile
She laid down her hand on him
She left the safe haven of help
And given into the life of leftovers
She settled for the first man to love her
She laid her body down to produce
She left the life so loved
And given into the softness of a shoulder
Nobody told her where to go

Hate will never heal

Hate will never heal, so let's hold each other tight
Before the world ends let's make love tonight
Not with our God given bodies but with our heart
Let's create the afternoon with our eyes and with our art
My life is full and so complete because you've entered it
To hate this feeling would be a sin so let's make love instead

Aunt Vira's Sausage Sandwiches

There isn't a thing so juicy and tangy
A taste of a sandwich that came from my auntie
A taste of a bite only countrymen know
You'd see it for a moment then it'd enter the hole
Your mouth would open and so would your stomach
If you go to her house, she'd give to all who want it
With mayo and mustard on each of the bread
To put it all together but then add the meat
So sizzling, so hot, so tender and red
A sandwich you wouldn't share, something you'd eat
Ain't nothing so good of a food that is handed
Then the food from my Aunt Vira, that good ole sausage sandwich

Dream on

Don't let it stop you from moving ahead
I won't forget you, I never will
If being on the beach is what you suggest
Always remember when the world stood still
Imagine love so black and brown put together
Hoping and wishing for something to last forever
Holding and kissing like all lover's do
Wishing upon a star that this dream come true
But for you, if the beach be something you prefer
I'll let you go, but always remember the night we both began to stir
Dream on my dear sweet Aly and never let it fade
For life is but a little thing and it won't always stay
Dream on my love, my forever girl, my life, my earth, my star
Forever you are, forever you'll be my dream which is afar

BROKEN STONE

A broken stone has created a storm
to bury the winters to keep you warm
To drown in pieces of dreams of hurt
A broken stone buried in the dirt
To company my sole a bitter cold
To store far later when the beat is old
A broken stone compared to my heart
Break my bones and in my grave I rot

ONE IN A MILLION

You have given me my dream
To sleep in winter and awake in the spring
you are my everything
My morning time, my night at 9
Thank you for being forever mine

WONDERFUL THINGS

After this long road of a lifelong lived
My dreams came true which he did give
First step to ambition, last step to truth
With more love in my heart ever since my youth
The sun rose high, fand the night grew fast
With faith still here the light will last

MY GRANDMA

She is gone, so far away
But the joy is still written upon your sweet face
Her smile, her warmth, her ever lasting voice
Has embedded a whisper entry upon your lips so moist
Her touch, her kiss, her memory that you remember
Will always be put upon your heart
Because her warmth outlasts the winter

IF YOU EVER LEAVE

If you left my side, I would die
If you left my side, I would cry
If you left me alone, I'd drift
Far away into a what if
If you left me here, I'd hurt
If you left me here in the first
I'd show your heart my lonely tear
If you were to ever leave me here

TWO HEARTS

One heart in this city
Another in the other
The day they came together
Is the day each found its lover

Many say I be wrong
But others say it be true
The lovers did not care
To them this was new

I LOVE YOU

Talking to you caused my wave to rise
We are on a cloud of an informal tide
You are my wave, the wave I will ride
I surf on your heart like my love is wide
On cloud nine, a surface to unknown
Created for you and I, we call this place home
My heart forgiven and shown to someone so new
For you I'll give it all something I'll always do
Trust in me and know that hurt lives no more
Loving you more than ever, more than you've loved before
Believe in me my love, I'll never leave
I exist because of you, you're the reason I breath
The reason for my existence, you are the reason why
The reason I write to your heart, to swear I'll never die

MY NEBRASKAN BEAUTY

With your hair of fire
And eyes of leaves
And lips of pink cotton
It's hard to breath
To taste your bod
To touch your skin
I feel upon your heart
And your soul within
Your hair of Irish fire
Your eyes of leaves to blow
Your lips so sweet of cotton pink
To cause my love to grow

A kiss of wet upon your ocean
To cause your wave to rise
To love you now and forever on
I'll do until the day I die

ONCE UPON A DAY

On a day in the fall
Where you fell in my arms
I remember that call
We both shared our charms
You spoke those beautiful words
Your voice took me to heaven
Where angels sing of birds
I fell in love within seconds
I made you smile and also laugh
I wish that day would never end
You gave me answers when I asked
And on that day a picture I send
You sent one too of your lovely face
An image of beauty I'll never erase
On a day in the fall, you shared your heart
And that is why I hope we never part
My dear sweet Laura, you've sent me free
One upon a day when it was you and me

THE CONFUSED PIECE

In your eyes you're a window
Silent bright and dark to answer
Door bells and knocks but you do not open
You are the only identical cancer
You hide and run but tears continue
Your disguise is powerless against my heart
You want to live within me
Be my puzzle and always be

SAVE ME

Lost soul surrounded by black day
Run away from light in the month of may
Hide and do not make a sound
Nor crawl but sit up upon a hard ground
You find words to speak
You find words to speak
Yet I do not understand lies
Your lost soul is very week
Like the small body of many flies
Stay here with me and keep the faith
Together, you and I we remain safe
Come out too darkness and promise to scream
With light of love your world is now free

WEB OF LOVE

Your heart is on a strong
A web of confusion to swirl
A line of love you bring
To spin contagiously around my world

A TREE ABOVE THE GRASS

Long life to live by dirt
So low to the earth yet still
So much to count and feel
I see why you get hurt
A place of birth, you move
And the wind will blow your motion
And life will grow in you
Until the day to be stolen
Long life you lived by dirt
It helps you grow and also feel
You cannot move but you bruise to hurt

Love is what you need to heal
I cover you with my arms
I stretch passion on your color
To protect you in weather of so much harm
You will never suffer
I am of you, still from the ground
I will not hurt you
I'll never let you down
Long life to live by thee
I will not flee
Peace be still, so I stay
I remain yours, till my last day

IN LOVE

I admire your work, your love if forever
It is all around and pursues life
You capture the sun and stars to set sail
If Paris be of wine this life I drink
My fire from this flower is felt with pleasure
To call you my own, I'd call you my wife
I dig deep into this love, may it not fail
To drown in this wide of life I'd sink
The sun in my skies and we are together
It is the ocean of waves I ride
Let his love be of color and not pale
In my heart and mind there is you
And I think, and I know that I am in love

About a Man I Knew

I remember it well, I remember his smell
His hair gave me chills when it entered my face
He cared for me more than anyone ever could
He is the one I will never erase
He would take me places I never knew I could go

We were so perfect together until the day came for snow
The first fall of it all caused a slide of the tire
He held on but the ice caused a fire
I remember it well, I remember that day
A day full of snow, only wish I could erase
He cared for me so dearly, so near to his heart I was
The man I knew I know gave me a deeper love
I will never understand why this world swallows souls
To harm my lover the way it did and took his heart away from me
The man that I knew is now gone but will always be free

Rise of Honor

Tonight, we fight, tonight we conquer the hate
Tonight, we love, tonight we open the gate
This field we fight upon will bare blood and headless hearts
I lift my hand to charge at the evil, for tonight I love
I will avenge my father's killer; I will show him what was
This world is not to shed a tear nor blood
So, take my hand my evil enemy and wash off the mud
We are neighbors not enemies so let us all stand as one
To venture deep into the hate to slay the one who killed the sun

No Ordinary Love Affair

The job was simple but also sweet
I did not know I'd fall at her feet
A rose with thorns to create this lust
I kissed her neck, her lips, her thighs
I wish this night would never die
She made me love her in one night
This affair, I sweat, will give me life
Her smell is on my skin and also the heart that beats
For miles I'd only walk, if she would walk with me
This love is not simple, the job was more than fair
I fell in love with a woman who made this Love affair

The Reddest Town Ever

There is a town I passed today, a town of only two
A town of pain and suffering, a town with less to do
A town of guns, a town of knives, a town of murder too
A town of who, a town of how, a town so red of shoes
The prints uncovered to match a 10, the size of Johny Jones
A man who yelled and kicked his wife, the lovely Connie Jones
This town of two, a town so red, a town that I passed through
Has marked a spot up in my life of the two I never knew
But red of red and death until they part has given the town a name
The name of some, of none, of one, the town of none to blame
For in that town the two are dead and the sun has changed to red
A story told of a town so cold, the Reddest of the red

A sleepy writer

I am so tired of typing; my fingers are crossed and still
I write instead to know my words are more than real
And yet I am still tired, I am wanting sleep
But I have to create the love, the life of every dream
I could write forever, and never yawn
But I am worn out and want to sleep until the break of dawn

I Wear the Mask

I hide from the world, and I hide from myself
I think of me as ugly and everyone else
I hide my scars and my frown for I cannot grin
I hide my pride and I hide my love, so pain is stuck within
I think I miss the old me, but I really don't know
I used to be full of life with an everlasting glow
But now I hide my face from you, I erase my loving soul
I hide with a mask and also the shadows of a love a long time ago

A Flock of Failures

Buried in the yard are prisoners of crimes
The dealers of many, my poetic rhymes
They cage them with wires and feed them their poison
The rage of a storm of a cloud cooled and moistened
The cells are cold of a billion hearts and dreams so shattered of glass
The tales are old of a billion truths and screams of a prisoners past
They roam the halls of prison walls until the doors are shut
A flock of failures within the walls have come to lift their cups
To toast to life, to toast to love, to toast to a brand new day
For in that flock, that sinful stock, the crimes will fade away

Lisbeth

If you look into her eyes, you are entering an eruption of fierce winds
Into the eyes of a mermaid so sweet with terrifying fins
Into the world of an Aztec goddess with fire in her eyes
But when they water, I see the daughter of a cloud of rainy skies
Beautiful and bold, petite yet young, she possesses a power within
The spark in the dark of a shark so feared when you strike her fin
Her eyes tell it all, her dark sullen eyes, they bring this world a storm
Her eyes of cold, her winter's snow, she stares to stop what's torn
I write to you my sweet small friend, a girl who gave me fear
For in her eyes I felt the pain, the pain I placed so near
Don't cry my love, don't shed a tear, don't wander without me close
Please smile for me, please, while I'm free to give your heart a rose
A heart so sweet, with eyes so calm, I caused your storm to fade
For in those eyes are erupted dreams of love which you have made

The Missing Money

I open the dryer, and look through my pocket,
And what do I find, my dirty bar chocolate
I look through the couch and search under it too
And what do I find, not my kangaroo

I figure maybe my brother, maybe he has a clue
I look through his drawer to discover a dirty shoe
I open the cabinets, and next comes the closet
And what do I find, my brown leather wallet

The Frame in my Head

The picture stuck in my head has held my pieces together
Imagine a world filled of her, with pieces of a feather
So soft, so gentle with delicate delights for all the world to see
A frame ashamed her love has changed but kept her love for me

We be but little children

We are small, no knowledge of left or right
But I write to tell you these things
We are a ball of yarn in a big world
And I continue to write about all of this
We fight, we kill, but we never hug after
I write furthermore of these things that we choose to ignore
What are we living for?
Why do we hate?
Words are in the way of the way that we live
Words get caught in the middle and causes the actions to give
I write about what we choose, what we have chosen
Why do we persist about what is unspoken?
We be but little infants, little children
We do not understand the ending of it all
We will stand or we will fall

Beans and Beer

After a long day of work and more work, I walk through the door to a
place I call home
I wander for a bit, lazy feeling, not knowing what I want to do or eat
My wife and kids are not around, they had left me all alone

I guess I'll open a can of beans and grab a beer and relax my feet
Not even a bowl nor a microwave, just a can, a spoon, and my dear cold
friend
I lay it down upon my bed, just me, my can, and my beer before bed

Light in Fire, Love in Water
Light in my love which has given me fire
For water to burst into silence and create such desire
I retire my thoughts of burning
To enter the satisfaction of water for my thirst
I will continue to live for the desire of fire within my heart
A place that the water ran deep to cause this depart
The end of hate and into the long-lasting system of love

My Beautiful Big Girl
From night to morning, I want to hold you close
With a body so plump it keeps me warm
From day to night, I keep you from harm
Because you are my delicate fluffy rose
You lift me up whether I'm down or not
If I could do the same, I'd possess the sweetest muffin
For you are the bread I place in the oven
And that is why to me you'll always be hot

If I Could Fly
If I could fly, I'd go to Paris, for we will always be
If I could fly, I'd travel the moon, for coolness of air is in you
If I could fly, I'd go to the bay, for you are there my sunny day
If I could fly, I'd go to the mountain top for higher love that will never stop
If I could fly, I'd travel the ocean to give to you my romantic explosion
If I could fly, I'd go to you, if I could fly, that's what I'd do

I Wish I Could

I wish I could go to China because they produce the most
I wish I could swim to Brazil, but I do not know how to float
I wish I could type faster, but my brain is a disaster
I wish I could drink like a fish, oh boy I wish
I wish I could dream forever for all dreams come true
I wish I could see you soon and one day be with you
I wish I could hold you close and never let you go
I wish I could grow a rose to resemble your gorgeous soul
I wish my love, I wish my girl, I wish my life with thee
Would be for real but not until I wake up from this dream

We Stand Alone

Just you and I are left to fight off the monsters
With the world closing in full of fire and coal
With a sword and a stone, we swing and we throw
To defeat the elite alone will be our ultimate goal
I adore the fight within you my love
No matter the obstacle you continue to swing
And in heaven my love, you'll grow your wings
And that is why I continue this fight
My dear beloved, my lover for life

Number 597

Number 597 at the 7/11 and boy I tell you, it's all a blessing
To be able to rhyme and write and share
Number 597 is the best I swear
From sunrise to sunset all I do is think of rhymes
Remembering the words and rehearsing the lines
With thoughts of a girl and dreams of a verb
It'd be to kiss her lips and to give her all my words

A Day by the tree

Driven for an hour and found our destination
At first there was one and then another
Looking for the weather man for the precipitation
Ducking our heads and looking for cover
A sound I heard was loud and fierce
The wind went one way then drastically another
We looked in the distance and used our ears
We spotted one and then it's lover
With feathers and such and claws so long
The king of the air with a roaring song
With arms expanded and eyes so sharp
It's voice so performed of the harp
Viewed by many and more other people
Today by the tree, we saw an eagle

The sound of pain

I wrote her a poem and also a letter
To make this life seem somewhat better
I wrote her a dream and also a line
And in that dream, she was mine
Her lips are still, and eyes are closed
And with her hair, her locks I'd hold
Her eyes were silent, her mouth was too
I tried to convince her but her anger grew
The death arose and love was broken
And in the end these words were spoken

I hope you are happy

Enjoy it all my love, I hope that you are happy there
With the water between your toes and the wind in your hair
Enjoy it all my dear, I hope that you are feeling free

With the waves in your ear, and the breeze between the trees
When you have done it all, over and over again
I hope that you continue to smile for a beautiful life my friend

The Scariest Sound

Tonight, is the worst night of my life
My girlfriend left me for a reason unknown
Tonight, would have been the night I asked her to be my wife
But not anymore because my beauty left me alone
She shook me to the core and broke our promise
Life is scary to shake the cage
I put in so much time to rewind an us to be honest
I fear that I am going to go in a rage
I flip the page to the next nightmare
And there she is, the love with the black hair
My beautiful disaster, my gorgeous stain
She is the cause of all this pain

Down by the Riverside

Down by the riverside where the kids would play
All but two by the riverside would play
The rocks would fly, and the water would splash
The fish would jump, and the kids would laugh
Shadows cover the light which sits on the waters
Hearing them playing, our sons and our daughters

I Dwell in Hell

The window was open for you to come inside
My presence was made but you chose to hide
Why create a wall between our hearts
What made you drown the ship from the ark
I felt you in my dreams, to scream loves name

But you fade away into another day, opposite of the same
You burned my existence when you left
I crawl into a hole, second book on the shelf
I fade away as well, I dwell in hell

One More Day

I see you; I feel you, my house is filled with pain
I feel you; I see you through this window pane
Do not slither into my life and drown my greed
For the reason is the season, and the thought is the need
The seed I bare, the hurt I wear, I tear away
Into a better love up above into a new day

No Fools Allowed

I wrote a rhyme in school, I told you I was fooled
I rose from the bottom to pull the top to the roof
I rose, I flew, I dreamt of you
I will not be schooled nor will I be fooled

God of Grace

God of grace please erase the rage
Lace the lines for all my rhymes
I worship you and no other god
You are the love who gave me this ride
Place it high and shine with every beam
Put me on the bench, as long as I'm on your team
God of my grace, empty this place
Hold me tightly and never escape
Forever in your heaven I will remain
For waters are cool and baptism is a must
Please give me grace and I'll love and trust

My Globe

Where is my father, where is my brother
When I was young, I was no brother
I had no siblings, and I had no friends
I created more hate with the help of a pen
I wrote down the page and climbed up the mountain
I did not stop until I finally found them
I opened my eyes and realized you
What did I terrorize when I met you
Pain, hurt deep, no heart, no soul
But love always exists and it made me whole
To fold, to flip, to flop I forgot
But I continue to write, my story is chopped

Love Me

I was a told story by one man, me
No soul knew my name but me
Be who you feel, feel who you are
I am not a zero, I am a star
Love is my name, God is my father
I will not have a dad, but I love my mother
Stay true to your thoughts and love all
I am the seasons created in the fall
My name is life, alliance of forever
Love me dearly, love me forever

My God

Only God will judge, only God has mercy
Only God be the glory and God loves me
Life is so loving, hard but lovely
I accept the pills, the pain, the hurt
I love you all, I create a saga soon
To hear me crawl I will surely do

To love, I have done, to rise high, like the sun
Thank you for my life
I live, I dream, I love

Love Alone

I am the one who you hate
I am the one who gave you the gate
I create the pill, still I open for you to feel
Stay humble and stay loved, I create the life
For you to steal, I will drink
I am drunk on you, I love your eyes
I love your skies and I am alone
I create the life of hate to steal your own

The path that I must take

The road not yet taken nor broken by teeth
I chip away the pieces beyond my belief
This path of life we walk will tear down our wall
But I will not close my ear to not hear the call
You see the tears of innocent eyes, heal them
Do not walk away from those skies, reveal them

All the Same

Into your eyes I have grown fruit and land
I inherit this life, the skies begin to plan
My tongue pierced with truth, with total loss
Of hate, of greed, I do not pay the cost
I harness love and embrace pain
For we are not enemies, we are the same
This fruit which grew, this voice
Has risen among those of choice
I celebrate with song and write with love
I embrace joy, pain, and the heavens above

Do Not Change

Do not change on me, do not believe the lie told deep
Stay and remain the love, before the pain find pipes to leak
I know that you are far away from me, and I know I feel pain
But I uplift the love you gave, the hope will remain
Until then I must continue to give the metaphors of love to your heart
I must continue to entertain the girl I met in the start

The Art

The body you have is something I'd love to grab with every stroke of my brush
My mind is a manifest of lust, and you are the canvas that I want to rush
I crush this lust into a life of love, the essence of this might be to much
I insist to write, to draw, to paint the woman that gave me this brush
I continue to dream, to paint the paragraphs upon this page
I and stuck into a world so romantic of a Romeo for rage
Not the same rage that you crave but the rage of the slave
I am yours to devour so taste the paste, the paste of my brush you cannot erase
For I am your painter, and I am your artist, most of the ones who will create

I feel you

The last time I went to this world I did not taste your love
I gave it my all, but you did not give me enough
I sacrificed the whole title to my life, the whole dream that I had in my mind
And you left me with the only thing that would be left to find
I found you on that winter snow, that day so cold
You were there to heal my body and to warm my soul
You kept me whole and held me tight that night
That one kiss on the cheek I remember
Until December was done, then you left in the blackest of months
I remember that day and cried the whole night
I will never forget the dream which became the worse horror ever

I felt you so close, and I still do, I feel you, I love you

For you the love of my broken heart, I will always cherish this deep love they can't ever undo

Drown my suicidal thoughts

Murder my mind and leave behind the whole destination of destructing my heart

For I am the creator of a sudden belief that love last forever and from the whole start

Drown my hate for myself and give me a wish, a hope, and a chance to succeed

I am down on both knees for you, for me as well because I do not want to go to hell

I do not want to end the last hope of poetry, I want to stand and be free

Can you be the end of the hate and list all of the love that I can continue to dwell

For the drowning of my thoughts are the ideal dream of every ending of a bad nightmare

This is the last tear that I will tear, yes, this is the last particular vibe I will have to share

In Between the Lines

From sunset to sundown, I showed you the regrets

With eyes wide open I caressed your gorgeous neck

With dark days to born suns, we rush into deep lust

With sheets felt on soft skin, deep becomes my thrust

I enter into the land where she is more moist

Crossing those rivers with a pleasurable voice

Your body is so amazing, I understand it all

I read between your thighs as your skin begin to crawl

From sundown I want your lips to set rise I want your eyes

Within the sheets and underneath I creep beneath to make you rise

I taste your fruit and devour the juice and send shivers down your spine

I've given this lust in depths so deep while in between your lines

The Shower

Come with me to this place
Where the dirt has no vacancy nor does a past relationship
This is a place of peace and space
Where an orchestra is performed by your beautiful lips
A place of waterfalls and rain
You can soak into the warmth and coolness of such a place
A place of the opposite of a stain
Where you and I will enjoy the wonderful embrace

The Times I Remember

I remember when we were small, we were just like you
Little babies in a bubble bath
The splashes and the noise gave our parents a clue
We were all bad
Asking for food every 30 minutes
And fighting over who's going to do the dishes
I remember when we were you, so precious and loud
We were cute until that all ran out
From laying in a lap to sitting in our own seat
I remember when the grocery lady was sweet
She'd give us a sticker and call us adorable
I remember the good times when everything was affordable
Because at that age everything was free
I remember the day when it was you and me

The tears she gave me

I wept away into the arms of an unknown lover
She swept away the life I had and entered the life of another
She left me with a promise to be mine again soon
I wept away for the unknown love who did not want to be my moon
I was her shine on the days so dark and within that joy I gave her light
She swept the tears into the bay to lay me rest and let me die

Today I write, tonight I dream of the lover who never showed her face
And in that face, I did not trace the absence she gives to quickly escape
She's gone from me, so far into the sea
My love for her was real and true
And in this love, she becomes silently
Among the dead, a forgotten tomb

Angels Do Not Fly

In that sunny land above the highest peak
That glow of a light so bright it shows
A land of white without faces or smiles
The longest of lands which stretches for miles
Bears the fruit so sweet to sale
An endless land of trees to tell
And in that land are birds to fly
So high they soar like never before
Below that land are other things
Which sits and stands and also sings
Such creatures are pretty and also sweet
With the tune of a harp their hearts will beat
A rose of a group with gorgeous looks
They sing, they clean, and also cook
With smiles so wide and legs so long
They create a debate for the ones who are strong
With eyes of the sea and the grass and the sands
These beauties are the cuties of the cutest in our land
I think they are from heaven for the angels they be
They possess the very image except without the wings

I guess she's gone

My dear sweet girl has drifted into a world of waters
She has left the dry land and emptied my arms
You are the loneliest shore that I have ever seen
The brownest of brown and my everything

You, my love, are so far gone and with an empty heart
You sail the ocean and crash into waves
Without the water or a sail, I too have crashed into this wave
You have given me the ultimate storm in my eyes
And in that sadness, I will cry the deepest cries
I guess you're gone, so far gone
I have to let this end, I have to let you remain
And in this departure, I remain alone

Roses are food for the Heart

Roses are red, for your bed and your belly
And violets of grapes like jam to feel like jelly
The roses of your hands and the pedals on your feet
To taste the reddest rose would fill me up complete
With arms open wide, and please keep hold the thorns
For I am but a Romeo and for you I adorn

Open Blinds

To peak out of the corner would be obvious and with danger
And in the middle would consider my life as a stranger
To pull the string would expose who I really am
And more above would cause me to fall for you
But down below when I look through the blinds so low
Would be the mystery when I finally find the way to propose
On bended knee I will ask thee to fill me whole
And in that room the blinds will open forever with all my soul

Piece of Paradise in Her Eyes

That little piece of hope within her eyes
That paradise is built within her skies
With the sweetest pie placed in my hand
I'd love to taste it any way I can
With a heart so warm I hold it close

And in that stare you give bears a rare rose
I love you and the beautiful heart that you have
I'll keep you here with me because it's you he gave
With eyes so pure and everlasting to me
I'd place that paradise deep into my forever dreams

Paralyzed

They used to run faster than the rivers and streams
With legs of fury, they'd burst with speed
Without a pilot they controlled the land
Until the day the Wright's took a stand
With a plan they mastered with wheels and wings
And busted the legs of hopes and dreams
Test after test to release the plan
To create more travel in the air for man
With a pilot in his seat and the wind at it's wings
They burst into air with the turbulence and speed
No more land, nor legs required
But with they're wings they continue higher
Up in the air, and never to land
With the paralyzed plane to release what was planned

The Day the Sun Stayed Asleep

Hurt and pain, a tremendous amount of pain
I could not breathe the way that I should
I do not think that I will ever be the same
My heart has sunken into a hole, and that is where I stood
You have taken my reason to live
You have taken my heart to crush it so
And why did you ask for more to give
Only to take my love and then let me go
My heart aches badly, it drowns down below
I cannot survive this; I thought you and I would be
But you have torn out this, the only good in me

And so, I depart from the world for years
which caused me to fade into a sleep full of tears
Never will I lift, nor will I enter into the wake to rise
For you are the dreadful gift, and the reason why my sun won't shine

My Girl Bee on Point

Never have I seen a beauty such as her
With lips so plump and hair of fur
With eyes so wide, so brown and true
With her bread so big and her pancakes too
So sweet of a woman, can't none compare
But look out below, there's something in the air
I told her to duck, but she moved towards it
My beauty must be crazy as if she wants to reward it
Then she had mentioned the bee is the reason
And I'm just wandering and also thinking
She further explained more about the buzzing in the air
She told me the reason and I thought that was fair
Now I understand why she's shaped so well
The bee from the air has touched her with a spell
My sweet Latina lady has been tricked to not disappoint
And now I see why my girl always bee on point

The other side of Heaven

I traveled there, only there is where I found her
She was laying on the beach with coconuts beside her
I thought of no other after the day I laid eyes on her
I have never seen a woman so special in my eyes
I have seen so many beautiful things but nothing as beautiful as her
In that place I have found my paradise
And in her eyes, I have found a place that will surround my heart
I hope to never part from this love that I feel
For in this Heaven her beauty is for real

My Faith

With all the pieces of my heart I love you
I know that you are far away into a better world
But I still think of you, and I know you do too
I will not let go of the memories of you and I my girl
God created us to be together and I believe it so
And for that reason, I will never let you go
Stay strong my dear sweet lady, and never forget us
The love that connects our love, our bond and our trust
Imagine the ocean flowing slow, as your hair does my love
Imagine the air, the wind, the sky, the flying of a dove
It is all you, only you whom will fill my heart with faith
Without you here and nowhere near, I'll continue to love this way

The Highest Place

I have never died and seen the light
But if I did, I'd love to see heaven
I could not travel to that dark place tonight
It would have to be the beautiful place of seven
On the 7th he remained still and gained all his strength
I wish to go to this place of peace the day I am erased
For when I leave, I'll release my things to whomever will take my place
God of love take me up, take me high and I will fly

To Love a Woman

To love a woman, you must submit
Let go of the ego and give it all to her alone
To love a woman, learn to forget
Let go of your past and know that it is gone
Hold onto her hard, stay close to her heart and mind
Cherish every second, because true love is hard to find

Love her deeply, so deep within the core of her soul
Love her forever, to love that girl give her the world

Jungle in the Gym

Where the court players play are some animalistic beasts
No matter the sport you play, never play at your least
Dominate the object and be the most valuable predator
Control what your mind is feeling and love the game forever
Sneak up on the ballers, do not let them win
Control the beast they made you and kill the monster within
Never give up the way you play and never give up the love for the game
For what you have within your love, will definitely and always remain

Just Play the Game

This is life, not a game
Don't rush into the love of fame
This is real, not a joke
Don't regret what you do, even if you choke
This is love, love the game
Don't ignore the voices for choices will be to blame
Just play the game

Deliver Me From Evilynn

On my way to work with a badge and my pen
Wondering if I have to watch her again
A lady name Evilynn who was mean as can be
She in 96 years old, but she looked like 103
She'd spit on my tablet and fart in the bed
And when it was time to eat, she'd always want to be fed
She'd spit out her dentures and murmur something bad
With a voice of a horse and she's still the worst nag

She would hit me with books and curse at me too
And if she became hungry her big butt would want more food
But Evilynn is old and of course she'll be cranky
She reminds me of my kinfolk, my mean ole auntie
I can't wait until my shift is up to be at home again
Lord, please watch over me and deliver me from Evilynn

I am here

Idaho has been good to me for years
So many lovers, so many tears
The mountains here could get cold in the winter
But in May we would cut the trees of timber
The flowers would bloom and so would the ladies
Because of my car, a dark red Mercedes
But I am here now, a place where there's peace
A life so beautiful, a town so sweet
I go home to visit, in Louisiana that is my home
But I am here, and this is where I belong
With you and the rays of sunlight God has made
So, I remain here, writing, under the cool shade

The Love I Give

I love to make you feel good inside, I love to fill your heart with joy
Your heart is pure within yourself and on the outside bears the light
And that is why, for you, my love will deploy
Deep into your heart, and forever in your eyes

On a Date with My Destiny

Let's travel to the ocean where the waves sail us far away
In that distant water we will enjoy the candles of the sun
And in the night, we will go underwater with the sting ray
For my love for you is strong and it has just begun
We swim to the stars where we are met by a comet

And in that wish, we kiss the sweetest kiss
So cool of a breeze from your lips our wetness will connect
And the smooth lining of your mouth is pure bliss
We leave the stars and land upon a cloud
And by that cloud is a gate of love and light
Such love, I wish to stay here with your smile
To see you happy is my dedication in life
On our next date I'd love to walk with you down the road
A road so long, a road which will not get old
The road of memories and obstacles and also pain
But don't fret, for this road will lead us to an eternity
Just you and I, my love; our true destiny

In the Fall of a Kiss
I'm sitting on a bench at school and there I saw her
Her face was tan of leaves, orange and yellow
The air was cool but if she be the soup I sip I'd stir
And so, with a nervous heart I said, "hello"
She slowly smiled and her eyes sailed into mine
Those lips, so pink, I could not resist
I leaned in to lower my head and caress her plum from the line
To meet with mine and enter there, a place where fell an endless kiss

The Silence of my Lamb
She sleeps and dreams of the love that we both lay upon
A cloud full of lives only cats would understand
She continues to travel into her dreams with a smile to pawn
For I will give it back to her when she travels back to this land
She will come back to me with open arms and endless kisses
Full of waters, rivers rushing rapidly and ultimate wishes
But for now, she dreams, she sleeps and within that sleep she is silent
Like a lamb over London my darlin' girl is my beautiful pilot

Letting Go of a Lie

It is hard to let go of you
I am tangled into your arms
I do not know what to do
I am open to you with both palms
What has caused you to lie to me
A promise told for the reason of hurt
You have drifted towards the sea
And I remain buried in the dirt
Do you even care where my heart lay
Letting go of a lie is hard to do
When time has passed so will the day
The day you tore my heart in two

Flowers in the Sky

This is by Aubrey Marie, the sky is so bright
At night the light will shine for us all
In sight the love and the colors are to fall
For flowers in the air are colorful tonight
The northern lights with colors or such
She says to put how she loves them much
The flowers will bring out the best in you
Shine bright tonight, while the colors are in bloom

Leave me for dead

My eyes bled red when you left me for dead.
She abandoned the only heart that mattered most.
The endless tear into my ship has poisoned my waters to drain me within
the crevasse of the ocean floor,
and in that departure towards my death will bear a forever sore.
A wound so deep it cuts the souls of heaven, and their tears are met with
mine.
They see the storm, my raindrops, my sadness, and in this storm, I will not

return but I will burn

I will bleed the reddest drop of a seed to bury me further into love

Do you miss me

It's been forever since I've last seen your body walk into my view

This day is new, but it is very incomplete without the presence of you

I have tried to get you out of my mind, but it does not work that way

True love is hard to find, and that's what I feel about you everyday

I think about you all the time, but do you do the same?

I do not want to torture your mind, but you're the one to blame

I know you're gone away from me, too far to see

But one question remains the same, do you miss me?

A pane in my glass

I sat by the window to look out to find you there

You sat by that same window looking up in the air

I'm still, and within my heart sits a rose

You fell for me and hit the glass slow

The fragments fell into me and caused me to bleed

With petals around me and the bend of a broken leaf

You've caused the glass to break into me

And then my rose to bend so vast

My vase was shattered for all to see

And you became the pane in my glass

To Remember the Day You Died

You laid in the hospital bed with your eyes dem

And so were the lights low to the levels

I was not there but I heard about them

And in that sadness became the devil's

Your torment of life has bled my eyes of tears

My heart ached so roughly with an endless snow

And while you lay in bed drowning my years

The ending of the sun began to let you go
Your eyes had shut, and a tear began to roll
My forever cry for God to appear but the precious life he stole
And so, this day I do not pray for mind has left my head
My darling girl, my endless rose, you lay lifelessly in bed

Lay on the Moon with Me

The air is cool tonight and your standing right in front of me
I hesitate to touch your star, but I do wait for your landing
I saved this spot for you and nobody else to be
Alone with me and you hesitate to fly my way
But with courage, I grab onto your hand to feel the coolness of you
I hope you do not deny the love that remains so true
I lay my head upon this moon for it is the place to rest
And that is why I need you there so lay with me my dear princess

The Fear of a Friday

If Friday could have never existed, then I would probably be fine
But on that morning, I saw the reason to never look behind
A figure in the dark with an unknown face but I knew that it was you
The one who left and tore the soul and broke my heart in two
Without a word nor a stare, those eyes looked away from me,
with eyes so cruel, within the jewel, became my enemy
A broken heart has left my body to bury itself so deep
A heart so lost, so out of place, it will not be complete
But do not worry and do not be sad, for I am doing better
I send to you this unopened love written on paper as a letter

The Necklace

On a night of promises I prepare a farewell to you
A goodbye unknowing my heart would tear in two
This night so sad I couldn't think to feel
To let you go nor to ever heal

With natural beauty upon your face you came to show me so
Without your makeup the sun sure shined with a ray of light known as a glow
Your hair came down for my hands to grab to caress it very slow
With time passing by I can't deny I began to feel you had to go

The 3 C's

There are many C's to see him but not by the sea
Not by the ocean but by the other C's
Cancer, car crash, and not going by the cross
It will be you who will regret what you've lost
The sea is filled with deadly dreams but not by everything
The C's to kill that will reveal the C for you and me
Which one are you, which will you be, the C of endless things
But without the cross we will be lost so always remember me

To persist

I do not persist with my eyes, but I do persist with my heart
It was nowhere sinful to hold you by the hand
Nor is it evil to love you from a farther land
But I persist to find you, I wish to capture your heart

Waiting for Pain

Give me a week, a week of complete silence
And then give me a month, for I can take that also
A year without you would be death to my soul
For my heart cannot take the distance nor the silence
So, give me death now and torcher me in the next life

To Crave a Girl I Knew

I noticed it all in you, from the beginning until end. I noticed the smell of
your lips as I look at the top caress the bottom. I noticed your eyes get thin
as you grin, and when you'd moan for my lips to press against your neck

I noticed when you grip against the wall so that my force can please your walls furthermore. As I venture my hands across your sands of lust I thrust my eyes into your soul, gathering all life and pure embrace. I notice when you think of me, for I too want to be with you at that moment. Your eyes are like a blade in the night, so sharp, so dark, so accurate for my every thought of you. I crave your scent, your every being I crave. I want you in my life forever and always

A Secret Kept Sealed

In the beginning it was her and I, we were never separate nor were we apart from each other. The complication was never there but we did have a spouse and we did have our own families. But for me, and for her, we were never separate. Our hearts were connected through words, through secret glances, and our hearts were connected through love in each other's arms, in our eyes, our minds were so deep for each other. It may be sinful to even think of the thought of her but with this secret kept deep I do not regret the day that I met her. If it be wrong to love her then I will go to hell with a heart full of fire, but I will have the forever memory of a woman who captured my heart and erupted it so with all the love in the world.

My Intentions with You

My intentions are pure at heart and from the start I could hear the song in her eyes which captured me so; I could not let go. I could not turn my eyes away from an ocean so blue, a sky so clear; I had to be near her smile. Without her I am lost, I am lost in her everyday. I will be lost in her eyes and in her smile; in her sky and her ocean, for I am in love with her. There are no limits to the love I hold for her. My intentions are and will always be to see her smile, to cause such an explosive happiness; and in her heart I will remain until she sends for me again. I will be forever lost, lost in her.

With Water so cool

With water so cool and love so warm
I embrace the word of Jesus' arms

With water so cool my mouth be moist
No sand nor dust can dry this voice
With water so cool, with love so true
I'm glad to feel and embrace it so, I'm so in love with you

My flight to the future
In the middle of the night, I had a fright
An adventurous night to begin a twelve-hour flight
At 6am I ventured from the couch
To the bathroom and away from being a grouch
I continued my flight without a pause
And in the middle of it all I began to crawl
Not knowing there would be weather so fierce
Always bad with good to cause this pain more tears
Eye to eye and hand to hand we stand all alone
Until this flight of endless fright softens til it's gone

The World We are In
Stay with what will guide you to the light
We stray, but do not be consumed in the night
Nor in the day, for the moon consumes the sun
Hold on to the light to image the world as one
Hold on to the sacrifice, embrace the blood he shed
Love the love that loved you first and banish all hatred

A Love Only Cigarette Smokers Will Understand
You, who will buy two packs a day, I see the love you have for them
You consume them without the hesitation to think of your death
Your love for them is rare and deep, you will make love to them until your
last breath
You light a fire under them and with that you create more desire to burn
that love
A love so deep; you kill this Romeo and Juliet of a story

For this will consume you both if you continue the life, you live
But you do not understand the love that is carried nor do you feel
A love so real, a forever desire, to burn the fire within

Scary Knights within the castle walls

Sir Lance became thy lover within moments
The haunting sword which slayed me so
The tip pierced my fearless opponents
To joust the heart with a final blow
Sir Lance has given thee blood on end
The haunting of the deadly blade
The tip to tear the love to bend
The sacrifices made
Sir Lance be me, the writer
Sir Lance be me, the dream
Sir Lance be me, the lover of lovers
The scariest knight I be

No Tomorrow

I am at the top, come with me and follow
Tip toe there and watch the monster swallow
I am what you fear, I am an empty hollow
Creep within the nearest day for there is no tomorrow

The Seven Men Who Saved My Twin

There are seven men whom I know
One is sweet with love of gold
Two be short without a toe
Three is sour at any hour
Four be scary and also hairy
Five is simple with an ingrown pimple
Six be silent with a tongue to pause
Seven be silly and born in Philly

But all be the ones who my twin did know
They knew my lil sis, the girl name Snow
She killed our stepmom, the one who was ugly
She ate from the apple because she was hungry
But the seven brought the prince to wake my sis up
He kissed her on the lips to give her the hiccups
When she finally woke up lil sis called the seven men
To make a story short, the lil seven ignored my twin
She left with the prince but the seven wanted her more
And that's the reason they ignored her, because the love was poor

The Day Mountain Home Died
Crushed and confused, I tore the very image of what we were
The Durango disappeared and my whole past two months became a blur
I do not miss the love that came over me towards you and your smile
But I do miss you and the image of a memory haunts for a while
The shattered heart and being crushed by this mountain of love cannot heal
I am forever in hurt because of the dirt within this love came and left me still
You took from me a gift given, a secret share of a care that is no longer there
And so, I will leave this here to disappear the way that you did the
morning's air
My mornings were nights my nights were too and inside I cried for I am dead
As days go on, I walk in hurt and in the dirt my death is fed
Of a heart so black, so lonely there, so forever dark with an endless tear
The day you see will be in me, to be the day my love left there

The Tree within me
The life is wide open
And my branches are grown
To a life so focused
And an affair unknown
With the leaves so green
And they fall before the wind
Will you grow for me

As if we'd begin
A life as one
And a love within this tree
With water and the sun
We will grow internally

The process is endless

Through it all I wonder about her
I used to cry but now I just sit and think
I used to imagine the trip to you arms
Through it all I know you are doing just fine
I used to hug you and hold you
I used to kiss your lips and stare at you all day
Through it all I will hold those thoughts deep
I used to wake up with the thought of you
I used to read to you and write as well
Through it all I wonder if you really cared
I used to imagine being with you
I used to dream of our hands connected
Through it all we are no longer joined and we are separate
I used to love you very much
I used to belong to your heart
Through it all you left me, and I write our last depart

In Hell I Remain

A star is born in the flame of no shame
I do not even remember her name
Low to the levels of lightening and hurt
I created this hell, now enjoy the dirt
The sin forgiven is not yet forgotten
And in this sin, I polish my thoughts
I sacrifice the heavens to enter what's rotten
To have in me, the doings and what nots

The flame is big and so are the levels
Now enter with me and embrace the devil

I Am the Poet
I am the one who has caused him to take her hand
I am the one who created love within the sand
I am the one who filled her eyes with a glow of blue
I am the one who gave the words to someone new
I am the one who caressed the heart with a word
I am the one who heard the song of a bird
I am the one who wrote the note without a quote
I am the one who gave the slave my love to tote
I am the one who loved you more and you know it
I am the one who will always write, the unknown poet

All Alone
The day has begun with my eyes wide and my heart closed shut
I fold my arms for there is no body to hold nor an image to cut
I do not talk anymore because the words will enter the ear to travel
Like the road ridden, the wheels spin to spit on me the pain of gravel
I do not expect much from the sun, so I sit in silence and enjoy the night
At least the darkness will keep me safe and in that place, I need no light
And when I die, do not cry for tears are waters for the cup to drink
And in this well I'll surely dwell for love to surrender and let me sink

Tempted Pleasure
Totally naked from the escape
Of life your lust will delegate
What depth of kisses she craves
To devour the pleasurable days
Such sin to sink into arms awaiting
To maintain the wetness of moistly playing

Her thighs so firm, so strong and soft
Her eyes to burn with calm jaws
So wet was her mouth, her tongue, her neck
For the deepest ocean will definitely forget
The places around, the sea thereof
The tide to turn and roll with love
And that is the sound her mountain makes
When her echo continues, and her valleys shake
That is the feeling her focus will learn
To shadow my love to take it's turn
To burn with passion for her body to move
Whatever it takes to show thee love
For your eyes do roll when my hands do sooth
For your skin is compared to thereof
Compared to the waters, the blades of the grass
The gentleness of a song and the winds which moves past

Bethany

For every stare that we share will be a kiss to compare
Looking into your eyes, I see the truth, no lies
They sparkle so bright, like a baby's night light
Your hair, I'll compare to a birds feather in the air
Your hair, your smile, it's like the long lasting Nile
Your voice is like a bird's, I love to hear all of your words
Your lips, I dream, are strawberries placed in cream
But your eyes are an adventurous disguise
For when they rise, there's a surprise about your dark sullen eyes
Your skin, how soft, let me touch your skin and your heart within
Your hugs, we have not shared, but in the future, they'll be compared
Your heart is the heat to anything sweet
Your eyes, your beautiful eyes are the reason why
The reason that the stars appear in the night sky
Your skin is like milk and as soft as silk
Your hands are warm things that I want to hold

I would rather have them than all the world's gold
But for a kiss, I will compare, for every stare that we share

The Kiss of Lust

Coming down the street of love I see
A big-hearted kiss seeking only me
My lips of moist I wish to kiss
Your lips, my forever, my only true bliss
To taste, to touch, I give you this
This lust, this love, an everlasting kiss
I'm in love with them
Your lips among the stems
Among all the leaves and among the roses
Among all of the flowers above
Just because I wouldn't close this
This wish, this list, this life I have
To kiss you there I'd have to grab
I'd have to hold, to gain your trust
To kiss your lips, I'd do for lust

Believe in me

I am sorry for the life I wasted
I threw away what you gave
I've bitten the fruit which was tasted
By evil unbroken which made the slave
I venture into the wilderness, into woods unknown
Now I am lost, and darkness I have to own
But stop and remember your faith
The love of him who gave your life
The strength he gave to win the race
To live for him, so do what is right
It is not the end, your life is not over
Win the fight and do what is right

Believe in me for I am he
I am he, so believe in me

Once upon a day

On a day in the fall
Where you fell in my arms
I remember that call
We both shared our charms
You spoke those beautiful words
Your voice took me to heaven
Where angels sing like birds
I fell in love within seconds
I made you smile and also laugh
I wished that day would never end
You gave me answers when I asked
And on that day a picture I sent
You sent one too, your lovely face
An image of beauty I'll never erase
On a day in the fall you shared your heart
And that is why I hope we never part
My dear sweet Laura, you have set me free
Once upon a day, when it was just you and me

The Journey Begins

In the middle of every footstep is a new beginning
Not knowing where you will go, you find yourself leading
Tracing every bit of doubt or enjoyment to continue
And in pursuing this journey you find something in you
The same step you took that brought you hope
A smile so big you climb without a string or rope
But you fly, you soar above all to see
That the footsteps you start with will always set you free

The Birds

Birds flock like a stock of corn
Until the chirping sounds like a horn
And fly high until wings break
How much longer will it take
To see those wings to color the blood
The color of red, the lightest mud
The tiny feet they have to stand
And with only wings, without your hands
To nest and rest their heads on sticks
On straw, on a tree, if only like me
The loudest of birds and the biggest of birds
The written animation of unthinkable words
A bird of heart and tears from hurt
The color of red, the bloodiest of dirt

Son of Darkness

For so on and so we fell into the forgotten
The fruit told the truth of a tree which was rotten
Rebirth of the darkness to bring forth the night
To kill every sunrise or beam which is light
Abandoned heart left a hand alone to fall
And in that void is where the son will crawl
Those broken hearts to beat broken bones
Of skulls which crush to bury them in stone
To come out dirty and filthy and cold
To live in darkness until we are old
But I am the one, the son of the dark
The reason there's no beam, no light or no spark

My Valley of Four

It's been four years since I've seen that snow
The chill down my back which melted it so

And the pond where our feet felt a cool touch
The captioning taken was never a rush
Walking in the forest and meadow and moist
And memory of the air which gave you a voice
Four years ago, when I fell into a crack
A valley so green, I will one day go back
Where the ice meets the pine, I will unwind the time
And one day venture the place I called mine
Where the water is between my toes
I will find that beautiful rose
When those days were lived, I look back at it all
Four years ago, until now I will wait for my call
Your voice, your valley, your beauty and grace
To erase this world of a dream which was so
To remember it well and never ever let go

Nightmares of an untold tear
Why do you haunt this feeling so wet
What has caused my land to flood
With a silent splash to surprise me yet
To wash my love with this mud
It came without warning or sound
It came like the river in pipes to leak
To fall to the ground
I bled the pond of hurt inside
I felt the lake of ware
I increase the fear of a monstrous tide
To reveal a love's nightmare

The Tool I Be
Once upon a night and once upon a day
My pen did write, and yet to say
I am the paper, the message from on high
To bring down to the earth, for it to multiply

I will be read, questioned, and taken
For good or bad reasons, I will be awakened
My hand must move, and my ink be filled
With expressions empowered with God's will
I am a tool, a message used to observe
Endure my every line, and also every word

Give Her Your All

Someone once told me that I cannot have them all
He gave me energy that day to pursue that catch
I capture hearts and enter them with all that I possess
I give into lust for love is the key and so I never stress
Words are what they want, and care is what they need
Give to them what you must and allow them everything
Why not go for what is hard and why not sacrifice
Give to them what's hard to give and she'll give paradise
Play the hand that stands for her and never allow defeat
For in those eyes, she hopes to be the only love you need

My Life is Love

I love more than love and that is why I must be alone
My love her was uncontrollable which sword couldn't break the stone
She is the first thought when I wake and the last when I sleep
The heat I feel when I'm near her body causes my heart to beat
My chocolate begins to melt for you and my love begins to leak
To give to you I'd forever do, to make this more than a dream

Bankroll

Save your money and stash it home
I got your back, you're not alone
With the heavy pockets and the wallets solid
I got your back more than you know
Do not forget how money grows

From tree to tree and in the snow
With every root begins some stash
And do not worry, I have your back
With cash of green and coin of gold
Everything is worth what it's sold
Control the bank and watch this roll
For green I bleed and for you a bankroll

The Blues I Got for You

Baby, I got colors in my box
And the main ones are the blues
I got the key so where's the lock
Because it's you I choose
I sing to keep from crying
I sing to only you
I sing because I'm trying
To keep from feeling blue

The Light in Her Eyes

Her light is fair and when she looks, she surely stares
I do not look towards the darkness because love exists in the light
So, within this light I see her smile, her eyes are always my stars
I feel it in my skin, and I feel her skin on mine
I smell the scent she carry's as if she is near me and not so far
I love her eyes; her name holds that to be true
My dear sweet pretty eyes of a girl I'll always love you
The light you hold and the light you possess keeps me so
Within your eyes are many skies of God's eternal glow

Aly Cat

There is no cat as cute as Aly
The sweetest cat whom I adore badly
A cat with fur which laid on me

To make my skin crawl rapidly
That darn cat caused my heart to sprout
And with those claws I sure did shout
A cat called Aly, a pretty sweet feline
A beauty full of fangs who I wish would be mine
But the cat called Aly is just a rhythm to me
A song from a mystery, the meow to my beat
If I ever met a cat in the streets or an alley
It would sure be the feline of mine that they call Aly

The Saddest Age

At this age we sit on the porch and watch the kids go by
Our house is filled with pictures and artificial flowers
With few words shared, we watch the rain begin to cry
And at that moment we tell our stories of how this all became ours
An age of us, just you and I will walk through these halls
To silence the time, I write a rhyme then begin to pause
And we sit on that same porch looking off into the young ones day
Remembering when we were younger, the times we would play
Time is gone and now we sit and stare into the new
All of that doesn't matter, I'm just glad I did it all with you

In these walls

In these walls are sounds and voices
Among them all were very few choices
I chose to hide and surrender the rage
To place a secret on the other side of this page
The collapse of the truth will one day reveal
The man within the wall whose body is concealed
The cry of the dead is what you hear
Listen closely with more than your ear
Understand the reason and then look more
Listen to the cries of the ones under the floor
I chose the choice to avenge the cries down below

The ones who tried to make a change but did not expose
Within the walls belongs a man, a demon so unknown
But if you fear the one you see imagine what is already gone
The many souls lost in time have come to show you the truth
Within the walls there is a man who took away our beautiful youth
I do not shame, nor do I regret the life I've taken away from here
To avenge these babes down below I'd do again without fear
Rest in peace precious souls and with this love I give
But in the walls, above them all, you remain but not to live

Hold My Love Until the End

Hold my love the way I'd hold you in the night
In bed we squeeze each other so tight
With pillows and sheets, we lay upon
But without those linens I'd still belong
To you and you alone I'd belong to
Hold this heart so that it beats for you
Hold my love the way I hold this dream
And in this sleep our souls will meet
To tear this love is impossible to do
Close your eyes and it'll remain us two
This simple thought of us connected so close
Is my image of this love with a red rose
For you I'd give to see you smile
And the smell of it all will travel for miles
The scent of my love for you is all over
The bed that we share will definitely uncover
For pedals are there and so is the scent
Of love and love and more to be present
Feel my heart, touch my skin, and never let this go
I feel your eyes upon my life, and I will hold you close
For in this love, I feel you there, and I will never leave
I hold you close, so very near, for us to always be

The Boot Sniffer

One day you will see that the boot sniffer was me
I walked in on a Wednesday night and sniffed those boots for free
While two were eating and the other with a buyer
I looked around the store for something to try on
Not knowing what to get, so I chose this belt
And then I saw the boots, they were sitting on the shelf
The cashier came to see what I liked
While the other two sat and watched with both eyes
I liked a pair that I thought would be for me
So, I sniffed one of them out of curiosity
The two girls laughed and so did she
I went to the hats hoping she'd come by me
And then it was time to ring me up, so she grabbed my things
To cash me out but I couldn't resist so I grabbed her pinky
She glared at me and made a smile, a smirk and then a wink
She grabbed my hand and held it close, for a minute or two I think
And sadly, so I had to go but I'll write this down to give her
A thought of me, the one she knew, her Wednesday night boot sniffer

My Life

Complicated and confused, my life is alive
Even though I made so many lies
I struggle to choose right so I stumble
I hurt you badly until you crumble
My faults will not be forgotten nor lost
So, for these evil deeds my life pays the cost
My life on a finger, in a world untold
I gave you hope, but my love was cold
No love at all, affection casted aside
My love, no love, no feelings left to hide
I am your future, and you are mine
So, I write to save God's grand design
I hurt because you hurt; a tear in the sky

These words are in my heart, so I cannot cry
But I try to bring forth truth to your eyes
So, I write from a heart with very little size
What does it mean, this ring that I have
This is my life that God gave to grab
I threw it away, I tossed it aside
All because of lust and my selfish pride
But no more to worry, my life is with two
Two plus one, and that one is you
What I will do will be seen
With time, let me show
This truth is all I'll ever need
To show you that I will not let go
Why do I write tonight? I write because of love
I care, I swallow, I taste this life
I write to you, whatever thereof
I write to you because you are my wife

Make Love

On this night I hope to taste your kisses
Your lips so soft, so smooth, so wet
I will travel down that endless road, so moist
And make my way into the taste of your tongue
On this night I will end up holding your body
Firmly, with you in my arms, I grasp onto paradise
Never have I ever wanted to taste something so sweet
On this night I whisper into your eyes
The stare of many promises that will leave you smiling
Making your skin crawl as my words travel to your ears
Warming your body with a fire you do not want to resist
So, on this night, with this kiss, I kiss your neck
To leave a mark, to embrace your taste
I surround you with thoughts and wants
I give your lips, your eyes, your body and your mind
My passion, my charm, my taste for you

On this night I will give desire, fire, and lust
On this night I embrace your lips
A taste sweeter than the sweetest flower
To devour you is to cause your flower to bloom
I cause you to melt as I lick your neck
To make you moan, to grasp onto me
To hold you close, I will cause you to want more
I travel my hands into places unknown
Such a place is sacred, but my wants are anxious
So, on this night I caress my body with yours
Make love to me with your mind, for on this night you are mine

Silly Love Needs Love Too

If your roses were red and your cheeks were too
I'd kiss you on them both until your lips turned blue
When your lips turn cold, I'd warm them up red
Until your mouth is open, for your stomach to be fed
When your stomach is full, and your lips are hot
And your roses are bright for the stars at night
When I've given you my all, and but all that I've got
I'd try to muster more to give until the day I rot

Dead Sky

The many pieces of you, I've scraped away two
Maybe more were taken, I pushed what's been shaken
I empty my thoughts of you, a memory left undone
Whatever happened to two, the nightmare has won
The demons appeared amongst us, with wings to spread of red eyes
With loud sounds given to thrust, from down below to the skies

Faith

I am not shackled nor am I afraid
I am free and not a slave

A man of many with problems of few
A man with little but I do have you
To fall to the ground, I've done before
To fall and stay I will do no more
Because of you I am here
Because of you I have no fear
For each day I live, I thank the lord for you
For each day he gives my dreams do come true
Cold cell I sleep in; I lay with the lord
Cold cell I eat in; I read his holt word
This paper is my friend, and I fill it with love
This paper has no end, so my words do not shove
The glow in me is our father and he shines his light
The glow you see appears in the day as it does in the night
My life is not my life' I live for him alone
My life is a life because he allows it and so I make it known
As beautiful as the day, you gave birth to me in May
As beautiful as this life I live, my heart I show, my heart I give
I shed a tear but not of fear
I shed a tear because I am here
Here with God, alive and well
Here with him, and not in a cell
I am not alone, nor will I give up
I am at home, a place where there is always love
When the time comes, I'll see you again
When the time comes, our smiles will never end
I am not shackled nor am I afraid
I am free and not a slave
A man of many with problems of few
A man with little but I do have you

My secret sailor

Once upon a dream I met a beautiful woman, no ordinary woman but she
was a sailor. She possessed a smile so sweet and eyes so pretty; I could not
take my eyes off such beauty.

She sailed to our shores and said she would stay for a while.
I was mesmerized by her scent and cultivated style. She has taken me to a
place in paradise, a place so unknown to my eyes. I could not get her out of
my mind, nor did I care to do so at any time. It was winter and the sea was
frozen, so she stayed.
For many nights we would sit and talk, and in my lap is where she lay. I
held her as if it was the last night that I would look upon her face.
Her body was warm, her lips were sweet, and her image is something I'll
never erase. As weeks went by, she told a tale, but this tale was a story
which will be true. She said she's leaving our island soon and I did not
know what to do. I thought of ways, so many thoughts, to keep her body
next to me; but spring will come, the ice will melt, and she will sail upon
the sea. An invitation was given to me by her to venture upon her land,
when I arrived, I stayed a distance because another had taken her hand.
She had a lover, a dominant sailor, whom I could not compete; I missed
that day to be with her and yes, my heart has stopped its beat. The final day
came for her to leave our shores as she told me so, I wish the day would
have frozen in time so that she could never go. But she left my sight and
ventured away to a land so far, far away. A land I must one day travel to see
and find my sailor upon the bay.

A dream by the shore

I am with you on the shore
And you are who I am doing this for
I think of you all the time, almost constant
Those eyes, those lips, your skin so soft
If only I can escape from these thoughts
Everything about you is perfect to me
I think of you a lot, almost constantly
So, I write about you day and night
Wishing you were here in my sight
We think about you daily, almost constant
Me and no one else, just me and my conscience
It bugs me so to ask what you are doing
And I start to think maybe she's moving

Maybe to be back with me once again
But a conscience is a thought, a feeling within
In reality you are there, and I am here
But I wish you were close; I wish you were near
My conscience so clueless, it bugs me more
Asking if you are on the beach or sailing back to my shores

I Must Let Her Go

Upon the bay I must not go, for life has taken a turn
Her words were poison with a promise so false to cause a burn
My heart she struck to stop my breath, to put our love aside
To leave the memories in the past, to run away and hide
I must not pursue this love I knew, I have to let it go
For in that past did come a snow and so my rose will grow no more
So, wash ashore this mission of love and gather all of your dreams
Because the day she went away would be the last best thing
I'll always remember and never forget the sailor that I knew
My forever love, from God above, goodbye and farewell to you

The Love I Let Go to Get Back to You

The day the sun came so did my last cry to leave my face
I erased the sadness to embrace the better days
Such days were gloomy and unaware of what to come
But God gave me strength and in that struggle the love won
I cannot imagine being without the one he gave to me
But this world will pass and move on one day eventually
I've loved so many loves in my life but none as much as you
My forever girl, my whole entire world, this line of a rhyme is true
I let her go to find the one I am truly destined for
And on that shore, I'll look no more for her love was not mine to store
I had to leave my sailor's dream to come to you and let it be
I hope this love will give me a chance and remain again to be with me

Never Give Up (Bobo and Mama)

In the winter there must have been 10 blizzards because the ocean is near my neck. I struggle to understand your forgiveness, but I guess I've been blind to your kind of love. The sound of the light turning on at night scared my sneaky thoughts. I haven't written in a while, but some days are good to be put on pause. On Friday I sit in a cloud of white on a day so cold with cloud pieces falling down from the sky to the ground not knowing is stress at its best, but didn't God tell us to trust the rest? He loves even the smallest creation so why not allow that water to fall into your mouth when the thirst is wanted? Do not shy away from an empty piece of paper. Make those dreams and thoughts come true. Do not stop living when a shoe is at your neck, do not back down when the devil is at your door. Look towards that ounce of light which burns into your heart.

Tears of a Thousand Hearts

Those tears are waves of waters
For lost sheep, poor sons, and daughters
To feed on rivers and lakes to join
Into a thousand eyes to continue going
The strength is there and the sea so wide
To combine those oceans, we dare to ride
This pain pierced deep and puncture for thirst
To shed more tears our tears will burst
Those drops of rain splash into puddles
To create such sound, we see in double
For tears do fall, the call of thousands
To one day dry and create an island
This pain won't stay, those tears will fade
Far into dust where we were once made
Those tears you feel will be felt no more
For those are the drops which were meant for us to pour

Milton Keynes UK
Ingram Content Group UK Ltd.
UKHW010645020624
443357UK00003B/72